Widower
to
Widower

Widower

to

Widower

Surviving the End of Your
Most Important Relationship

Fred Colby

Front Range Press
Fort Collins, Colorado

Published by Front Range Press

Library of Congress Control Number: 2018903006
Library of Congress Cataloging-in-Publication Data

Colby, Fred, 1948– author
Title: Widower to widower: surviving the end of your most important relationship / Fred Colby
Fort Collins, CO : Front Range Press [2018]
Identifiers:
ISBN-13: 978-1-7321159-1-0
Nonfiction – Death & Dying, Grief, Bereavement, Grief Therapy, Widowers – Loss (Psychology) – Family Relationships – Title

Revised Edition

Book Design and Production: Front Range Press
Cover Design – Jeff Piaski
Front Cover Frame Photo - halfpoint/depositphotos
Front Cover Wedding Photo – Michael Arthur, Photographer
Back Cover Photo – Lindsey Parrish Photography
Interior photos – Fred Colby
All rights reserved.

Dedication

In memory of Theresa Colby,
a wonderful loving wife, friend, and lover
who made my life and me so much better.

Acknowledgments

With gratitude to:

My loving daughters, Charlene and Jennifer,

My sister, Ann, who encouraged and supported me during the writing of this book

My therapist, Mia Towbin, who suggested I write this book and supported me through the process.

Alexandra Kennedy, MA, MFT, author of *The Infinite Thread: Healing Relationships Beyond Loss*, who reviewed my early book drafts and provided invaluable insights.

My fellow widower, Robert Devereaux, who joined me in starting our Men's Grief Group and supported my writing.

Pathways, which provided a safe place for me during the grieving process and offered counseling support to my family.

Many other friends and family members who made my grieving more bearable and who encouraged me to write this book.

TABLE OF CONTENTS

SECTION 3 – AFTER DEEP GRIEVING

INTRODUCTION

After losing your life partner, there are moments—many of them in fact—when you may doubt your very sanity. For most of us, that triggers the "flight or fight" reaction. If you fight (confront) it, your chances of coming through this intact are much improved. If you try to run away from it, you may only be delaying the inevitable grieving process.

The greatest fear I had during the earliest stages of my grief was that I was going crazy, was losing all control over my thoughts, and that I might make decisions harming me, my family and my friends. That included suicidal thoughts. This scared the hell out of me and I became desperate to find answers, so I could avoid making bad life choices. I quickly found those answers would be hard to find, and that resources for widowers were minimal and often of dubious value.

This book is my response to frustration I experienced during this search. I have done my best to compile the most vital information I could find on the widower experience into this one book, so the reader does not have to go to as many sources for answers as I had to do.

Blogging helped me to process my experience as it was happening. I share these blogs from Caring Bridge (caringbridge.org, a site that facilitates your connection with friends and family at a time of loss) throughout the book in chronological fashion—starting from the time I discovered there was nothing else the medical profession could do for Theresa, my wife of 45 years.

Following this introduction, I break down my journey and what I learned into sections designed to address the experience of losing one's spouse. I cover how I coped with my loss, as well as recommendations on how one can meet and overcome the many challenges which lay before a widower as he enters his new reality. In preparing to write this book I documented my experience through the blogs, read many books and articles, talked to numerous widowers, spoke with therapists, and gathered stories through counseling groups, including a Men's Grief Group which I helped to start at our local hospice. *Widower to Widower* is the culmination of my journey to date, and my search for answers.

From the beginning, I struggled with the "widower" label; it asked me to accept the death of my wife. Each widower's experience may vary from mine, dependent on many factors such as length of marriage, depth of your connection to your wife, and/or how dependent you and your wife were on each other. Other relevant factors can include cultural background, depth and closeness of your support circle, how you were brought up, and your religious convictions.

In addition to quotes from other widowers, my personal observations and lessons-learned are supported by references, and insights from Licensed Marriage & Family Therapists who have extensive skill in counseling those grieving the loss of a loved one. This provides the reader with some guidance as to the commonality of my experiences with those encountered by other widowers, as well as an overview of different experiences one might incur.

My book is not meant to be the final word on the experience of widowers, but rather an exposition of one man's experience and how understanding that might help you to deal with your own loss.

The frustration I experienced while trying to find materials that would be helpful to me often left me floundering. Visits to online and brick and mortar bookstores, online searches for relevant articles, and perusal of the few resources I did find, failed to provide answers. My therapist, who consulted with others as well, also could not find much that was helpful.

Through this book I wanted to include many of the critical issues that you will not find addressed in other publications. What I wrote here can often be raw and brutal at times, much like the grieving process itself.

Widower: When Men are Left Alone (Campbell & Silverman, 1996; out of print) was the only other book I found that covered some of these issues well. It includes interviews with twenty widowers, with commentary by a Licensed Clinical Social Worker after each chapter. Unfortunately, it is not only an old book with some outdated information, but it also did not go in depth on many topics. Online articles by widowers provided some help on specific topics. I've listed the best of these resources later in this book.

I spoke with other widowers to confirm that mine was not a unique journey but was in fact similar in many respects to their journey as well. The entry into grief is intense and harsh, and I could not see how I could write this book without being totally honest about the experience.

Sadly, many men do not turn to counseling for help when they need it most. Widowers are currently underserved by counseling groups and agencies. There are very few male counselors to turn to, and many female counselors are uncomfortable working with widowers, in part because of the anger and sexual components of their healing process.

When you consider the impact of these issues upon your psyche and well-being it is rather amazing that there is little research on the topics I cover here.

I am the expert only on my own experience. It is important to note that each widower's experience is unique. There will be common threads and shared experiences, but each must find their own path. We must learn from each other, to realize that we are not going crazy, and to know that we can survive this experience.

Besides helping my fellow widowers, their friends and family, I hope and pray that this book finds its way into the hands of some well-qualified researchers who will conduct further studies on these topics so grief counselors in this field can be provided with more resources to help their widower clients.

To all those who follow me and seek answers during their painful journey into widower-hood, I dedicate this book.

Fred Colby

SECTION 1

PREPARING FOR

WIFE'S PASSING

Chapter 1

My Introduction to Grief

The loss of my wife was the most traumatic experience that I have ever had. Research covered later in this book shows that the stress that widowers experience is the base against which all other stressful events are measured. When Theresa passed, I lost my wife, best friend, lover, and companion in all things. Like so many men, many of my social connections were through and dependent upon her. Widowers are at very high risk of incurring life-threatening physical, emotional, and psychological challenges after the loss of their spouse—a fact I explore later.

A Wife, Lover, and Partner Worth Grieving For

I met my wife, Theresa, 47 years before her death. We knew very quickly that we wanted to be together forever. Our brief meeting at a party at a friend's house occurred while she and friends stopped by on their way to a big party in Los Angeles. I zeroed in on this beautiful, exotic girl of nineteen and got her phone number before she left with her friends just thirty minutes after arriving.

We had an unlikely whirlwind romance, as we were literally from opposite sides of the track. I was from a wealthy northern enclave in San Diego, while she lived in a mostly Hispanic blue-collar community in Southern San Diego. Our very different backgrounds did not stop us, though there were several "learning opportunities" along the way.

She worked full-time at PacBell while I toiled away at the local Mesa Community College trying to make up for twice dropping out of other colleges.

The first time we told her parents that we planned to marry, they pretty much ignored us, so we moved in together and lived the idyllic life in San Diego's Pacific Beach community. Around six months later, her parents accepted the idea of our marrying and we planned a big wedding, which took place on the shores of Coronado in San Diego. Two bands, lots of home cooked Mexican food, and much dancing kept us busy until we later escaped to Disneyland for our one-day honeymoon before I started attending college at Claremont McKenna College in the Los Angeles area.

Theresa and I were attracted to each other in large part because we each brought qualities that made us stronger as a couple. Theresa was the empathetic loving wife who was patient with my obtuseness and insensitivities. She was also intuitive about people and situations, which I learned to appreciate. Over time I learned to take on a few of her qualities, which made me a much better and stronger person.

In turn, Theresa took on some of my qualities and became a more independent and stronger woman. My self-confidence, focus on solving problems, and independence rubbed off on her over time. Together we became a very strong team that supported, strengthened, and deeply loved each other. It was a passionate love during the early years, but, over time it developed into something much deeper and more special. We never stopped loving each other or enjoying each other in every way, including in the bedroom.

Theresa was that special woman whom everyone gravitated towards because she was unconditionally loving, unselfish in sharing of herself, and unwilling to engage in attacks on others. She expressed joy in life through her sparkling eyes and in how she got excited by the smallest things. Everyone around her would be sucked into her vortex and enjoy life just a little bit more because they knew her and spent time with her.

Her beautiful character showed through in all her relationships and bound others to her in ways which benefitted everyone. She was the one making jam for friends, sending cards to everyone she cared about, offering to take a neighbor to the doctor, writing the checks to help her

7

friend's' causes, and stopping and taking the time to talk to—and listen to—someone who needed help. She brought people into her groups who might otherwise have been left out and alone. These people loved her unreservedly and were loyal to her to the end.

For me, she was the foundation of my being, the one who taught me how to become a better person, the one who stuck by me when I failed or lost a job, the one who always supported and encouraged me, the one who loved me when I could not love myself, and the one whose example I appreciated and adored.

I remember when I was around thirty, in a job I hated, and I was drinking way too much. Theresa never confronted me with anger or disappointment, but rather encouraged and supported me as I struggled to improve through a return to church and then through seeking new employment. Her love and lack of condemnation allowed me the space to heal and become a better man.

We went through many other changes in our lives that taught us how to support each other unreservedly. This instilled confidence in each of us and allowed us to build a solid and wonderful life full of re-wards and love. This in turn allowed us to become good parents and to instill many of the same qualities in our children and grandchildren. Theresa was, and is, a wonderful model for all of us.

I always told others how fortunate I was to have her in my life. I would sometimes compare my life to a chair with four legs: my wife, my faith, my job, and my family. I was soon to find out what life would be like with two of those legs (wife and job) gone, and one (faith) in crisis. Trying to keep a one-legged chair upright was about as impossible as keeping my life from collapsing after her passing.

Beginning of the End for Theresa

Theresa was diagnosed with uterine cancer about a year prior to her death. On December 31st, she underwent surgery to take nodes to test for cancer. That was followed by a hysterectomy, six rounds of chemo-therapy treatment, a blood infusion, and the first five of a planned twenty-five radiation treatments.

When she failed to recover from the chemo sessions and exhibited extreme tiredness instead of recovering as predicted, she and I sensed that things might not be going the way they were supposed to go.

We understood from the medical professionals that the cancer was likely gone, but she was not responding well to treatment. After the chemo was completed, I took her in for a blood transfusion to address her continuing exhaustion. We walked into the hospital for the treatment, but I had to take her out in a wheelchair.

The next day she had trouble remembering things from earlier that morning and the previous day. That night she had a mild stroke and paramedics took her to the hospital for emergency treatment.

While there, the doctors ran a series of tests and scans to determine what was going wrong. They found that an even more virulent and very different form of cancer had spread rapidly to her kidneys and liver.

The next morning, while still in the hospital, her doctor gave us the news there was nothing else they could do to help her. At that point we knew she would die within weeks if not days. This was the real beginning of my grieving process, the time when I accepted that she would no longer be with me. Up to that point I had held out hope that she would survive, and I had been relatively optimistic about the outcome.

I clearly remember breaking down into full sobbing mode in an alcove of her room while I called my daughters to give them the news. I could not stop! It took a while before I could pull myself together and go to my wife to provide the support she so desperately needed.

She was still in the hospital when my daughters and I gathered around her to discuss next steps. While sad and hurting from that point forward, we entered a stage of making what seemed at the time to be carefully thought out decisions about how we would handle all of this.

The Caring Bridge Journal entries woven into this book pick up the narrative from that point. It provides a window into my personal journey through much of the grieving process, which continues to this day.

I have left in a few comments from family, friends, and acquaintances where I thought they were relevant and would allow the reader to better understand the grieving process. I hope these comments help the reader to decide whether this type of journaling or blogging might be of value to them, their family members, and their friends. I found it very therapeutic for both myself and those who continued to read them long after Theresa's passing.

The journal becomes a written record of your personal experience which you can look back on in the future when you want to remember each moment more vividly. I found this invaluable as I progressed through the grieving process. My memory would play tricks on me, so a record written at the time of the experience became invaluable.

Prior to or following each of the book's Caring Bridge entries, I discuss it in more detail, along with lessons learned. I also added specifics which were too personal or sensitive to share with family and friends at that time. Many of these lessons became clearer to me during bi-weekly counseling sessions which I began about two weeks after my wife passed. I was fortunate to have a counselor who was empathetic and not afraid of the more pronounced manifestations and reactions which I had during the grieving process.

One thing that helped me through the process was an ability to laugh at my experiences. This allowed me and the counselor to look at these experiences and reactions more objectively instead of my wallowing in a pit of doubt and fear, which can often aggravate symptoms and prevent the progression of a healing process.

One conclusion I can share with confidence is that you'd better buckle up for a rough ride, because there is no way to avoid it. Some may delay it, but not many escape it.

No matter how much you read on grieving, your experience may be different. I hope this book prepares you for the journey ahead, and that it provides some assurance you are not going crazy.

Chapter 2

Illness & Death

Do it right and save yourself from a lifetime of regrets.

G rieving the loss of your wife will make you question your sanity, your values, your humanity, and the self-image that you have spent decades building—with the help of your wife.

The emotional and intellectual preparation you need to have at this stage is both daunting and necessary. You are about to feel as though you have been run over by a freight train. Once the devastation hits, it can be nearly impossible for days, weeks, months, and even a year to be well enough to deal with the most basic tasks. I have yet to talk to a widower who was not deeply affected by his loss.

For me, the grief experience was like the story of Jacob (Genesis 32: 22-32) wrestling with an angel through a long night. During his struggle, Jacob's hip comes out of joint; he still prevails. The angel then gives his blessing, renaming him Israel, *"for you have striven with God and with men, and have prevailed."* Jacob's character is transformed by this experience.

Like Jacob, I found myself in a heroic struggle, and an endless wrestling match with my grief. My grief was painful and did not diminish, but, if I were to survive I had to see it through.

Because I stuck it out, even when wounded (both physically and emotionally), I could honor my wife with my grief, and emerge as a stronger and better person. In my view, if I had tried to avoid the struggle I would have done an injustice to my 45-year marriage, and not have survived as well as I did. My success was a testimony to my wife and our great relationship.

To help me through this struggle I was fortunate to have a great hospice in the area, and I soon called them for counseling support. I also identified those among my family and friends I could call upon when in the depths of my grieving.

One theme I hear frequently from other men (and women) is the regret over not being able to say goodbye properly, not being able to tell their spouse how much they loved them, and not helping their spouse enough to bring closure for them before moving on. Some of the widowers I met lost their wives overnight, such as one whose wife died in his arms while on a camping trip in the wilderness. The suddenness of it was an acute shock to his system.

Another regret I hear repeatedly is about not bringing their spouse home for their final days. Everyone I have talked to, who did bring their spouse home, felt that it was the right decision.

In our experience, no decision was as meaningful as the one to bring my wife home for her final days. When I went to bed in an empty house the night after she went into the hospital, I was kept awake by the feeling tearing at my chest that *I needed to bring her home, that she belonged home, that the hospital was not the right place for her to die.*

In the hospital, interruptions were the norm every hour or two, rest was impossible, and visits difficult to coordinate, not to mention the constant blood drawing, blood pressure tests, and so on. When I went to the hospital the next morning and told her that I wanted to bring her home, she cried and was in total agreement with this decision.

My two daughters and I went to work to determine which hospice to use, and quickly decided that nonprofit Pathways Hospice in Larimer County, Colorado was the best choice in our area. Their reputation was great, they were close and convenient, and they responded quickly. Much of the expense was covered by Medicare, thus reducing stress on our budget.

Within three hours of calling them, they delivered all the equipment (bed, bedpan, wheelchair, portable toilet, sheets, and other items) to our house. Other area hospices were for-profit businesses that charged higher fees, were not as well regarded, and not as customer friendly as Pathways.

Their staff arrived that evening to explain everything to me and my daughters. The next day after I brought my wife home, a nurse, social worker, and aide contacted us or stopped by. They came by every day except one over the next few days. Included with their supplies were pain medications (for example, morphine with instructions) prescribed by her doctor, as the pain became increasingly unbearable.

At home, my daughters and I could give her all the attention, love, and support she needed. We talked things through with her and took personal care of my wife in a way for which I will always be grateful. Assisting with feeding, bathing, medications, and trips to the bathroom, as well as explaining what was going on and discussing things important to her were just a few of the ways we could support her.

We scheduled her many friends for brief visits. They were all very appreciative. Ultimately, my wife said goodbye to everyone she wanted to see except one friend who was driving out to visit her. That night after her last goodbye she snored loudly (a common occurrence I am told as death approaches). I was exhausted and set the alarm, so I could take a brief nap, not knowing the implications of her deep snoring.

Waking up before the alarm went off two hours later, I immediately noticed a difference in her breathing. I knew right away that she was near the end. I was there to hold her hand, stroke her arms, sing to her, and encourage her with words to the effect that it was okay for her to move on—that we all loved her.

As I stroked her arm I could hear her breathe, sharp inhalations as if the body was making last attempts to capture enough oxygen to continue its existence. It seemed to me that there were no exhalations, only inhalations, as if the body could only take, but had nothing left to give in this world. Then her breathing just stopped and I knew she was gone. For about ten minutes or so I continued to stroke her arm, to give her encouragement, and to say my goodbyes. Her body remained warm, but I knew that it was now an "it", and not my wonderful wife, Theresa.

She was gone. Forever! Her parting had been relatively peaceful and pain free.

It was a sacred moment for both of us. That moment cannot ever be replaced by anything else. The hospice helped to make it all possible. I did not break down into sobbing at this point as a sort of numb shocked state settled in while I was doing what had to be done after her passing. I accepted her passing almost stoically, knowing that her pain had ended and that that the situation was now completely out of my control.

After putting on some of our favorite music, I called my daughters and they came over to say their last goodbyes. Theresa and I listened to this beautiful instrumental music, *Journeys* (Windham Hills Classics), every time we drove down along the Poudre River near Fort Collins. It spoke to me so clearly about our past journeys together. I hoped it was helping her on her new passage.

The hospice sent a doctor to document the death and dispose of all remaining medications within an hour of my calling them. They soon contacted the funeral service company we had selected so they could come over when we wanted them to pick up the body. They were prompt, thorough, and considerate. Within two hours of her death, these issues were all addressed.

> **Alternate Experience**: Others may prefer to leave
> the body in place at home for a period to say goodbye
> until it feels right to let it go.

The next day my daughters and I went to a funeral service provider to make all the cremation arrangements and to say our last goodbyes to my wife and their mother. As I kissed her cold forehead and placed one of her "Remembering You" stamps into her hand, I just knew that she was no longer there, and that the cold lifeless body was just that—a body and not her. It was painful, but at this point I was just numb and unable to express myself beyond a tear or two. One daughter joined me in the room for the last goodbye, while another chose not to. This was the beginning of realizing how differently each of us would experience the upcoming grief.

> **Alternate Experience**: There are choices to be made
> at the funeral parlor even when you chose the crema-
> tion option. Do you want the ashes? Do you want a

container for them, such as a vase or box? Do you want to include certain items to be cremated with her (for example, flowers, a favorite dress, a special book, rosary beads)? Do you want to have a viewing of the body before it is cremated? How many death certificates do you need? It is difficult to make these decisions; however, you must deal with them unless you have others willing to take these tasks on for you.

Your wife, like mine, may experience a period of illness before passing. If you have the "luxury" of this time, make the most of it and plan ahead. Your heart and soul will tell you, "No!" because you want to believe that she will get better, and that to believe anything else will guarantee her death. Your mind must overtake your heart long enough to be practical. Making these preparations reflects the respect you have for her as well as yourself.

Review insurance, investments, assets, wills, trusts, bank accounts, and any other legal and financial documents to ensure they are all in order. If not, talk to the banks, accountants, and lawyers to make sure it is all done properly, and get her signature on anything needing it before it is too late. Otherwise you will have a nightmare process of cleaning it all up by yourself without her signatures.

• Role of Hospice

Hospice care can come in two forms: a hospice facility providing care for terminally ill patients, or in-home support to create a caring environment for a loved one who is dying. The focus here is on in-home care.

Before signing up for an in-home hospice program, understand the role that hospice professionals play. They are not there 24/7 for you; in fact, they are likely to be at your home for only an hour or two at most each day. Sometimes, in longer stays at home, you may not see them for a couple days at a time.

Besides equipment, they can provide all that you will need in the following areas:

• training on how use the equipment,

- how and when to administer medications,
- nursing assistance,
- personal care training and assistance,
- counseling for yourself and family members,
- religious support if requested, and,
- training and advice on what to expect and how to deal with each situation.

If you choose a hospice program, you and your family must be prepared to provide all the daily care and support that your spouse will require, such as feeding, providing water, and personal care, including bathing, help getting to and from bathroom or portable toilet, changing sheets if needed, diaper changes as needed, and so on. You will also be responsible for medications and monitoring the person's condition, watching for changes and reporting them.

Our experience with doing all of this was fairly brief, as Theresa passed just six days after coming home. Others, such as one of my neighbors, may have an extended period of a year or more with declining health making the care of your loved one more difficult. When this occurs, you may want to consider hiring additional help from your hospice provider. This can become very expensive, so you should consider all the available options. The more you can rely upon family and close friends the more you can control the costs. Medicare is quite strict about what it will and will not cover. So, you are likely to end up bearing some of the additional costs by yourself.

Like everyone else, I wondered if I was up to the task of taking care of my wife's personal needs. Well, I surprised myself with how easily I slipped into the role of a caregiver and did it willingly. If you love someone or just plain care for people, you will be able to handle it—and because you handle it you will feel good about yourself and the support you provided to your loved one. Your regrets will diminish dramatically because you did everything you could for your spouse.

• How to Use the Caring Bridge Website

Caring Bridge (www.caringbridge.org) is a website that is designed specifically to serve families which have a loved one who is:
- going through an extended illness,
- expected to die due to illness, or
- recently passed away.

Instead of making numerous phone calls, email updates, or text messages, we could enter the email address of everyone important to Theresa, me and my family. Our family and friends were immediately notified of our new personal Caring Bridge webpage.

After that, they can sign up to receive notification of any updates (journal entries/blogs) that you add to the page. This allows everyone to stay informed of the loved one's status, receive notification of significant changes and visitation schedules, and to see a list of items on how they can help, for example, to provide meals, contribute to caregiving, and run errands. We shared personal entries; but, you can have them be more factual in nature. Photos can be added to both the journal entries and to a photo page.

Visitors to our Caring Bridge web page could:
- add commentary to our posts,
- view all the photos we uploaded to the site,
- pay tribute to Theresa,
- sign our guestbook, and
- view a calendar to check upcoming plans.

Caring Bridge does ask for donations from you and your visitors but does not require it. Several of our friends and family members chose to make donations to them. The service is invaluable and saves you and your family from much of the stress that comes with trying to keep everyone informed and up to date. If your family and friends are spread out across the country, it is particularly helpful to use this service.

It allowed us to also have a little distance between us and our local visitors while experiencing the therapeutic benefits of sharing information. We were able to instantaneously have positive and supportive feedback from our friends and family.

I warn you that each time you explain the status of your wife, the funeral arrangements, and so on, a little bit of your soul is torn away from you, and a little more pain enters your life.

Trust me, there will be plenty of pain without the added burden of keeping everyone informed individually, so I recommend taking full advantage of Caring Bridge or a similar web site.

The following are examples of the postings we did before my wife's passing to give you an idea of the value of using this service.

Caring Bridge #1: Theresa Home Again
by Fred Colby, June 25, 2015

First off, thank you all for your amazing expressions of love and support. Theresa and I deeply appreciate it. We brought her home today after a crazy series of events and days this past week. She is resting comfortably with my sister reading to her as I set up this account.

We will post updates periodically here, so everyone can see them. Don't expect morbid accounts here, you know that is not Theresa or me. We love you all and appreciate all you have and will do for her and me.

Please limit phone calls for now as there are so many of you it is hard to speak with everyone at this time. We will post some information for those who live locally and want to help as to times for visits, etc. Emails are welcome as we can access them as time allows.

Comments from Caring Bridge readers (we would read these to my wife and they brought her much comfort)

*Thanks for keeping us posted Fred – please give a big hug and lots of love to Theresa from her San Diego/Colorado friend. —*Lynn A.

Glad to hear you are at home. All of you are in our thoughts and prayers. If there is anything you need please let us know. We love you! — Tina G.

Good morning Theresa! You are in my thoughts and prayers and I hope you can feel the love I'm emailing your way! I will be over to see you very soon!!! —Margie E.

Theresa – so glad to hear you are home! I am looking forward to visiting with you during my road trip. I am ready for a BIG hug from my BFF from 4th grade! Love you too Fred. —Lin M.

Fred, I had not reached out first as I know how hard, hectic and difficult all this is. Second, I just don't have the magical words to say. I'm with you all in spirit. My love and prayers are with you all. —Ana B.

Oh Fred, Thank you so much for getting ahold of me... I did not know things had gone so far as this seems to say. Please give her all our love! I will continue keep you all in my prayers. Seems like only yesterday, we were there and sharing such fun times. Love you! —Rita H.

Caring Bridge #2: Sleeping Well
by Fred Colby, June 26, 2015

Theresa is sleeping and resting well after all the hubbub in the hospital. Lots of love and support has been coming her way. Her phone is no longer working, just burnt out last night. (I later realized how prophetic this was) So if you need to contact us specifically please use Fred, Charlene, or Jennifer's email or this site as we review it regularly. Theresa's email is still up, but I do not check it as frequently.

If your immediate family has at least one member who loves to write and communicates openly with everyone, that is the one to be the lead on the Caring Bridge entries. Others may like to participate as well; but try to limit this to those closest to your spouse and you, those you can trust to write about your family's experiences openly. I would suggest limiting it to two or three writing the entries as there may be too much going on, confusion about who is to write what, and overlap in what is said by different writers.

In our case, one daughter and I took the lead, with me writing the lion's share of the posts. I found it therapeutic and helpful to processing my grief and thoughts. It was a great vehicle for expressing thoughts about my wife, for letting others share in my grief, and for celebrating all of my wife's great attributes and accomplishments.

The entries here are to serve as one example of how you might use the web site, as well as introduce you to some of the thought processes that I and my family went through during and after my wife's passing. You will also get a feel for how our friends and family members used the "Comment" function to share their thoughts back with all of us, to support us, and to help celebrate Theresa's life.

Caring Bridge #3: Mama Colby
by Charlene O (daughter), June 26, 2015

Mrs. Colby, Mama Colby, Mother Theresa. Jennifer and I know our mom has played a motherly role in many lives over the years so we know this news is weighing very heavily on everyone's heart right now.

Theresa is the type of person that after meeting her you want to hug her, spend lots of time with her, and in some cases, possibly be adopted by her. Her kindness, patience, selflessness and gratitude are infinite. We truly appreciate all your support during this time. Keep those prayers coming, we want nothing more than for her to fail miserably at Hospice, to be kicked out for improving so much and to have many more memorable and happy years ahead of her. Our family is in no way ready to say goodbye to this amazing woman. But we will be making the most of every day.

As many of you know, my mom is a very talented card maker. If you would like to send her a card, I would be glad to collect them, and the family will read them to her. My sister and I plan to decorate the family room with all the cards. She appreciates every kind note, visit and call. In true Theresa fashion, she is more concerned about her family than herself now. We remind her not to worry about us and to let us take care of her. The family will discuss needs in the home today and will post meal and visit openings on this website as soon as possible.

Comments (a selected few to give a sense of the many we received)

I've had many happy times shared with "Mama Thewsa," (as I am fond of calling her). We had many laughs. We had tons of fun making our very own (or copied from our teachers) greeting cards. Those times are treasured as you are treasured and love by many TC! Love you Mama Thewsa! XOXO — Row S.

I have never met anyone who takes so much pleasure in making others happy. She looked on with delight as others ate a meal she took hours to cook, not even thinking to take any for herself. This is an overused phrase that couldn't be more appropriate... the world truly would be a better place if there were more people like Theresa. —Chad O.

Charlene... what a lovely encapsulation of the selfless spirit of your dear mom. How blessed the entire Colby clan has been to be graced with Theresa's joy, love and sharing over all these years. —Kate C.

Thank you so much, Charlene, for a beautiful tribute for a beautiful lady. She loves her family so much, and yet always makes time for her friends. I have saved every handmade card she sent to me. — Lin M.

Caring Bridge #4: Thanks & Visits
by Fred Colby, June 27, 2015

We are grateful for the support shown to Theresa and our family. Those of you who have been able to come by have seen the sparkle in Theresa's eyes when she saw you.
Though speech is difficult for her, she enjoys the talks and attention

from those she loves. And special thanks to the amazing Tina B for bringing a feast for our family last night that should see us through lunches & dinners today.

Our neighbors planned a family meal for Sunday for us. It is nice to not be worrying about that stuff and being able to concentrate on supporting our dear Theresa.

She remains, as always, thinking of others first... making sure we return wigs, stamping items, and other things to their rightful owners. Our youngest grandchild, Keira, 10 months old, never fails to elicit a smile and eye twinkle as do our other grandchildren. Family and friends are making this a little more bearable, so thank you all.

Comments (A sampling)

I also am so grateful for these updates and pictures, Fred and girls. This site is wonderful to keep us all posted and to get a quick message to Theresa. Give her a hug for me this morning. —Lin M.

Our prayers are with Theresa, Fred and family. When YiHua and I moved into our new home on Marian St. in Milwaukie, OR in 2005. We were fortunate to be Theresa and Fred's neighbors. It didn't take long before Fred & Theresa knew everyone on our street. Thank you for teaching YiHua how to make jam. Love, Jim and YiHua — Jim R.

It is so good to be connected this way. I loved seeing all the beautiful photos this morning. Each one telling an amazing story. It is true that love is her essence and family is her greatest joy. —Sharon K.

Lots of love, prayers and good wishes. Knowing Fred, we are certain the entire family and extended friend and spiritual family is providing all the love and support possible. —Anna and Richard Y.

- ## Creating Memorials to Your Wife

We found Caring Bridge offered us a way to let our family and friends know how they could honor Theresa by making donations in her memory to causes dear and near either to us or to her. Many wanted a tangible way to support us by making such a contribution. In our case, we wanted to express our gratitude to Pathways Hospice for being such an immense help during Theresa's passing.

For those who cannot be there with you, they can leave a message under the online Caring Bridge "Guestbook" Section. We saved and then printed out an PDF of all the online comments to put into a scrapbook that her four grandchildren and the rest of us could look at to remember her. We felt that all the loving comments will help them to remember her as the extraordinary role model she was, an example to emulate in their lives. The scrapbook together with the donations in her honor became living memorials for all of us to share in.

Caring Bridge #5: Donations in Honor of Theresa
by Fred Colby, June 27, 2015

Some of you have been asking about who they can donate to in honor of Theresa. Please consider support for Pathways Hospice here in Fort Collins. They are helping us through this ordeal. They are a

23

well-respected nonprofit which covers only a portion of the costs for these services through Medicare reimbursement, so any support you offer will help to defray their additional expenses incurred while helping Theresa and others.

- ## Some Tips for You & Family

Offers to Help: Friends and family offered to assist us, but both we and they often had no idea of how they could help. I was fortunate to have children and siblings who could help, and these became my go-to team for the daily care of Theresa. If you are not so fortunate, there may be a few reliable friends who have experience as a caretaker, who you can rely upon to assist with the personal care.

Your Health: As I learned, more than ever, it is critical that you take care of yourself during this ordeal by allowing for some time away from the home if possible, even if it is just running innocuous errands. I took the time to shower, dress, eat, exercise, and talk to my friends. You will dramatically improve your ability to support your spouse if you are rested, feel good physically, and are not in a constant state of distress.

Meeting Her Wishes and Helping Her to Not Worry: One incident is engraved on my mind: While my wife was in the hospital a masseuse came into Theresa's room and offered to give her a massage. She gladly accepted the offer even though neither of us was inclined towards massages. She really enjoyed it and felt much better.

The next day the masseuse came in and made the same offer. My wife was not feeling up to it. The masseuse then turned to me and she offered me a massage.

As I was experiencing much stress and tension in my shoulders, neck, and back I decided to accept the offer. As the masseuse gave me the massage, I glanced up to see my wife looking at me with tears of gratitude in her eyes. She was so grateful that I had accepted the offer, and for how my act of accepting the help indicated that I would take care of myself. And of course, it once again served as a very real reminder of how much she loved me and was worried about how I was going to handle all of this. These kinds of moments were so powerful and will stay with me forever.

I learned to take the time to talk to my wife as much as possible before she passed. We talked about the kids, grandkids, family members, her friends, and anything else that I knew was important to her.

I gave her the opportunity to share her thoughts with me while she could, including steps she wanted me to take after she passed such as funeral arrangements, disposal of her ashes, returning things she borrowed, distribution of her things, final goodbyes, and the such. This experience taught me that the more you can resolve while she can voice her thoughts, the more you will rest easy after her passing, even if the things she tells you would not be your first choice in terms of importance or what action to take.

The more I learn about the experiences of other widowers from talking to them or reading their stories, the more I realize how different each person's experience will be. In my wife's case, she was very concerned that all things be put right before she passed, usually thinking of others first, as was her norm. This included directions on what to do with her craft room supplies to returning borrowed items to friends. Others may experience a complete disengagement from these types of minutiae and not want to talk about such things.

However, I do recommend that you let your spouse see that you are going to take care of yourself. It will ease her fears about you and help improve your ability to be okay after she passes! I know of several cases where the wife told her husband to remarry after she was gone, even sometimes suggesting a specific woman for him to marry.

Those who are passing, especially when they have been the main source of love or income, may spend some time during their last days, weeks, and months worrying about everyone they are leaving behind. They want to know that everyone will be okay, that they have fulfilled all their obligations, and promises. They may express a desire to pass with no regrets!

Grandchildren Goodbyes: If possible, I suggest providing the grandchildren an opportunity to say goodbye as it does help with the grieving process down the road. It's okay if they are unsure about how to act or how to talk with grandmother. Provide them with a little bit of direction, but allow them to express their goodbyes in their own way such as make a drawing, a card or write a letter to give to her when they visit her.

Talking to a Widower: This portion of the book is meant for those of you who want to better understand or help someone who is about to or has recently lost his wife. Unless you are an experienced grief counselor, don't give into your natural urges and start giving advice on how he should deal with his wife's death.

I found that others helped by letting me find my own solutions in my own way. Others helped me most by focusing on being supportive, by asking about my wife, by letting me tell the story—I must have told mine over a hundred times—and by offering to help with practical things such as meals, cleaning the house, picking up the groceries, and mowing the lawn.

My emotional state was raw, and the best thing others gave me is a caring friend who listened and was supportive. Yes, I went out for beers with my friends, and yes, I would tear up often, or be hyper-emotional and make weird statements, but these were good friends and they supported me and did not react negatively to all of this.

It helped to have that interaction with others who would let me be who I was at that moment, and not worry about presenting the macho tough guy image.

I recommend that if a widower needs to cry, let him cry and know that it is okay to cry. Let him know he is not crazy if he shares some of his emotions, delusions, fears, and concerns with you. One of the great fears I had during this process was that I was going crazy. If he does ask for help, the best thing you can offer is support for him to enter counseling when he feels ready to talk to someone.

So many people recommend getting a pet, but there are long term implications of bringing a pet into someone's home. But, certainly there is therapeutic value in having a pet visit the home if he is open to the visit. This may over time result in him choosing to get a pet of his choice.

• The Passing of Your Wife

A single person is missing for you, and the whole world seems empty.
Joan Didion, *The Year of Magical Thinking*

Nothing can really prepare you for the moment when your spouse passes on. Nothing can prepare you for the shock, numbness, physical pain, and emotional responses that you will experience. What you can do, is to do everything within your power to make her passing as painless and smooth for her as is possible. I suggest that *this is the only thing you should be focused on during her last weeks, days, and hours.*

If you do this right, your regrets, doubts, and all the would'ves, could'ves, and should'ves will be greatly diminished. This will help you to avoid sinking into the depths of self-condemnation and allow you to focus on the grieving process in a much healthier way, which will in turn help with your healing process.

After my wife's passing, my daughters and I felt that we had done everything we could to help Theresa during her transition. We had no regrets, no arguments, no sense of things left undone.

But, I still had some things that may bug me forever. For example, I wonder if I could have noticed her deteriorating health a year before she was diagnosed with cancer. The sense that I did all that I could do was a huge weight off my shoulders, though. This, in turn, allowed my children and I to grieve together, without questioning every moment up to her passing.

The following Caring Bridge entries trace the last three days of my wife's life and how we prepared for it through memories and sharing and alerting every one of the coming event.

Caring Bridge #6: The Theresa I Remember
by Fred Colby, June 27, 2015

This new photo of Mother Theresa (sent by a friend) is the Theresa I remember, love, and keep in my heart. Fun, witty, and beautiful both inside and out. How was I so lucky to land such a great catch??

We had 47 great years together, 45 of them married. We brought National City and La Jolla together for our wedding with a Mexican and a Rock band, both played for free due to connections to her family.

Many I am sure thought it would never last, but I can testify that it has been a long and wonderful friendship that just happened to produce two gorgeous daughters, three beautiful granddaughters, and one energetic and handsome grandson.

We could not have asked for more!! I can only wish the same to all of you who have loved and supported us!

Comments (A sampling)

Oh Dad, this is so sweet. Jennifer and I are so lucky to have been raised in such a loving home. You set a great example for us of what a marriage could be and we appreciate that. — Charlene O.

My beautiful Mama Theresa: What an inspiration you have been in my life. You welcomed me with a hug the first time I met you and you have been "mothering" me ever since. You have no idea what a compliment it was to have you call me your other daughter. My tribute to you will be to try and be a better person, more like you the rest of my life. — Char S.

All I can say is that Theresa is a beautiful person both inside and out. Her smile and laugh are contagious. She was caring and loving to help the troops – she sent a card to my grandson when he was stationed in Afghanistan. A true friend – there is no one like her! — Lynn A.

Caring Bridge #7: Quiet Time
by Fred Colby, June 28, 2015

    Our family has just decided that it would be best to have no more visitors from this time forward. We are at that point where we need to provide Theresa with the quietest and most peaceful setting possible as she prepares to move on.

    We thank you all for your understanding, and for all your love and support...Theresa has heard all the wonderful messages and is so grateful. We will continue to read these to her as time permits.

    Fred, Jennifer, and Charlene

Comments (A sampling)

The entire Colby family is in my thoughts and prayers. A special hug for you, Fred. — Robert B.

Theresa, please know that you are in my thoughts and prayers. It was wonderful to be able to get to know you over the last 2 years my friend. God bless you and thank you for your friendship. — Love, Terri

Our hearts stretch out to you, Theresa, and family. Please know that we are here for all of you. Memories of wonderful times with you keep popping up. — Tony & Jan H.

All of our love and prayers to you and your family. Theresa is such a special lady and we are all better for knowing her. —Tina B.

Please tell Theresa how much our whole family has enjoyed knowing her over the years. Know that Kari and I as well as all three kids pray for you daily. Let us what we can do for you. Anything! — Josh F.

I'm so glad Theresa is surrounded by such family love and protective-ness. Wish I was there to hold her hand and tell her how much she's always meant to me. She's always had that big smile, mischievous sparkle in her eye, and open heart for everyone, making each of us feel special. My love to all of you. — Ann C.

Caring Bridge #8: Theresa Resting Peacefully
by Fred Colby, June 29, 2015

Theresa continues to rest peacefully, surrounded by her children and husband. We have had great support from Pathways Hospice as she continues this journey. We will never be able to thank everyone enough for all the expressions of love and support for this very special mother, wife, and friend who made all our lives a little better. We have not lacked for food and drink, with our refrigerator and counters over-flowing. With additional family arriving tonight, it will all be put to good use, and will relieve us of worrying about shopping, cooking, etc.... so thank you all!!

Caring Bridge #9: Theresa Moving On
by Fred Colby, June 30, 2015

Our beautiful wife, mother and friend has moved on to her new experience with all your and our love and support. She left us at 11:30 p.m. this previous evening. It was a gradual, quiet peaceful departure. I was fortunate to be by her side holding her hand, reading Psalms and hymns to her, and just loving her as her time came. I am so grateful for having this opportunity to be with her. Our daughters came over immediately after her passing to share a few moments with her.

The love we and Theresa received during the past few days has made this all easier. We were able to reach that point of acceptance, to let her go in peace as she had already decided to do.

True to her nature, Theresa waited until everyone had an opportunity to visit her, to say their goodbyes and she said hers to them. Your love gave her the strength to move forward. She knew we would be taken care of and continue to experience the love she had expressed to us every day. We are so fortunate to have had her in our lives.

31

As the pictures that we have shared so aptly illustrate... she truly was a saint and instead of going to Las Vegas this time, she will be going to a much much better place.

Thank you all. Love

Fred, Jennifer, and Charlene

Comments (A sampling)

Dearest Fred, Charlene, Jenn & extended family.... Had been thinking about Theresa all day. From her we all learned so much about the true nature of unconditional love. It is her ongoing legacy to us all. So grateful Fred, that you found her, married her, and brought her into our collective experience. And that her girls, grandkids, and extended family were blessed with her mothering presence. — Kate C.

Dear Charlene and all your family and loved ones, I'm glad that you had the time to say what you wanted to say and be there for her and each other in her final days. God be with all of you in this transition time and may you find all the Peace you want in the days ahead. — Marilyn R.

What a sweetheart she was, how reassuring it must have been for her to be so surrounded by the love of the three of you. Thanks for your courage in sharing your journey with us. Much love — Ann C.

Fred, Jennifer and Charlene, All of you are in our thoughts and prayers during this difficult time. I was blessed to call this amazing lady my friend. She made me a better person by just being around her. She never had a bad word to say about anyone. — Michelle P.

Charlene and family, we are so deeply saddened for your loss. We are pleased to know that she was surrounded by love and family – not only through this final stage, but throughout her life. We are inspired by the love and unity of your family. — Claudia & Eduardo S.

Dear Fred and Family... Know you are in our thoughts and prayers. I am so lucky to have gotten to know Theresa and she will always be with us, when we get together we will remember her smile and talent she brought to us. God needed a special Angel... — Tina G.

Dearest Fred and girls – Know that you are in my heart, and my prayers as you struggle with your grief and sorrow. She was such a blessing to so many. She will forever be remembered. — Linda P.

Fred & Girls We are told that we are just gifts on this earth and I have experienced that some of our most precious gifts just aren't with us long enough!!! Theresa was indeed a "breath of fresh air," loving and talented gift to me and so many. RIP, our sweet Theresa. —Carol F.

Hi Fred and girls. As I read this post I am so grateful that you were there to share the moment. The love that your family has for each other and the willingness to share with others is Amazing. Thank you for reminding us all. — Ranea H.

SECTION 2

COPING WITH

DEEP GRIEVING

Chapter 3

The Aftermath – What Now?

It will never be the same again.
Joe Maio
Men's Grief Group Founder at Pikes Peak
Hospice and Palliative Care (Feb. 2, 2016)

There is nothing that you can compare to with the aftermath of the loss of a close loved one, especially a long time loving spouse. That is not to say that other things like war are not just as traumatic, the difference is that you, the surviving husband, are alone in how you are impacted, alone in your grief, and affected in a way which is not really understood by anyone else except other widowers. The next chapters outline in some detail the immediate impacts upon one man, myself, during this experience.

- ## Immediate Impact on Me and Family

After her passing, all of us closest to my wife went into a period of shock. We were going about the daily business of making arrangements for the cremation, notifying family and friends, and responding to the sympathetic outreach from many people, but we were numb to everything around us. We could do what we absolutely had to do, and make critical decisions, but in between these must-do tasks, we pretty much shut down and could not think things through or hold onto a single thought very long. At times, we avoided confronting our new reality as it seemed surreal at best during the initial period.

My children and grandchildren were as deeply affected as I was. The intensity of the grieving may vary depending upon how close your family was geographically and emotionally. Children, especially young children, have the added challenge of not being sure of how to react, as this may be their first exposure to the loss of a close loved one. Mine were often looking to me and their parents for indicators of how to react.

I lost my father when I was six years old. While at the dinner table with my family after his death, I asked, "If dad is dead, why aren't you crying? Why aren't we sad?" These comments have stuck with me ever since. Though the adults in the room did not react to my queries at the time, I still remember and regret these insensitive remarks to this day. For years I agonized over them.

My questions say volumes about my recognition at a very early age that the Germanic upbringing of my mother caused her to be unable to express emotions openly. Though loving, she was limited in her ability to express empathy. I and my five siblings all struggled with this throughout our lives. I believe that her inability to express some of her sorrow openly made it more difficult for all of us as we moved on after my father's death.

Be aware that your children and/or grandchildren are in a hyper-sensitive state and will remember things about this experience that you may quickly dismiss. I found it best if I was supportive and loving in all my interactions with them. I avoided adding to their burden by responding negatively to their inquiries. They are naturally inquisitive and want to know what happened, why it happened, and how they should react. What I learned is that the more loving and supportive you can be, the better they will be able to process their grief, and the fewer regrets you will have later. I strongly recommend appropriate counseling for children and grandchildren. Grief counselors who have some experience in working with children can help both your children and grandchildren to process the grief.

• Including Children in Decisions and Tasks

If like me you have children, include them in decisions and tasks. I think it's critical. They needed to feel good about their participation, about how they helped their mom (or dad) to make this transition as smoothly and painlessly as is possible, and good about having shown their mom how much they loved her. It also helped to bond us as a family for the challenges laying ahead, especially the grief and helping each other through it.

My daughters came to our house every day to help and to discuss issues needing resolution. They assisted in any way they could.

They helped with gathering information on area hospices, funeral parlor and cremation options, and other services. They took the lead in arranging a "Celebration of Life" event that we did at a local restaurant, including:

- Getting copies of photos of my wife for everyone
- Creating packets of flower seeds for guests to plant in her memory along with photos and sayings for guests to take home after the Celebration of Life.
- Arranging for the food and beverages at the restaurant
- Putting together our guest list and notifying everyone
- Creating a guest book for the event
- Working to finalize table and food arrangements

After the event one daughter and her husband helped to create thank you cards which we sent out to all our guests and those who helped us out before and after my wife's passing. They continued to check in on their Dad and to help me out wherever possible. This support helped me tremendously to get through the tough times and to break up the depression and monotony of the many days spent inside grieving.

We arrived at an arrangement where I would simply let them know if I was having a "funk day" and they would then give me the space to grieve alone for that day. Sometimes you just do not feel like doing anything or talking to anyone. My daughters were very respectful of my need for privacy on those days, and I would do the same for them.

- ## Sharing with Friends and Family

We found it to be therapeutic and rewarding to document and memorialize our thoughts about Theresa and our life together, and about what we were going through during this time on Caring Bridge. This allowed our family and friends to participate in the grieving, which helped them too, and encouraged them to remain engaged and helping us through this process. Some widows and widowers I came to know just closed all the doors and kept everyone out; this can just aggravate the more negative symptoms you are about to go through.

I found that being hugged, fed, loved and supported went a long way towards the eventual healing that I needed to experience to become a whole person again. It was therapeutic for me (and others) every time I verbalized in writing or in voice my experience and my love for my wife. Yes, you will eventually tire of repeating the story, but until then go ahead and share and share until you tire of it. Here is an example of how I shared with others on Caring Bridge two days after her death.

Caring Bridge #10: Remembering Theresa
by Fred Colby, July 2, 2015

While we are still all numb over the loss of Theresa from our every-day lives, and while we still have our moments of tearful remembering of this amazing woman, we all have been strengthened by your out-pouring of love and support.

We cannot express our gratitude enough for your help during these past few days. We know Theresa wouldn't want us moping around in sorrow, but, she would be honored to be remembered fondly and with love.

For those of us closest to her we speak of the need to honor her by emulating her in every aspect of our lives. We call it the WWTD, that is to ask ourselves, "What Would Theresa Do," in any circumstance, a way to personalize the "What Would Jesus Do" saying in a way that we can identify with on a daily basis. As you all know, Theresa would treat everyone with kindness and unstinting love.

The only thing Theresa could not tolerate was intolerance. As one friend said, if you said something inappropriate that gave offence to others, she could give you that look that let you know it was inappro-priate (I know, I got that look often). In my 47 years with Theresa, I hardly ever heard her speak ill of anyone. She accepted everyone as they were, and just loved them as she did her own children. She did not judge, and she was unselfish in that she would give of her time to help anyone anytime.

She got immense joy out of helping others, whether it was a grand-child or the new person she just met on the street. She taught me to be more generous, more open, more patient, and more loving. I will miss her constant guidance as well as her embrace, I will miss holding her hand which fit so perfectly in mine, and I will miss being able to share daily experiences with her, but, I know that going forward I can best feel her presence by expressing the same qualities as she did in every way possible.

So many of you express wonderful qualities that attracted Theresa to you and that kept you in her life. That makes knowing you and shar-ing this experience with you an opportunity to continue to feel her presence with us through you. We thank you for being there for us and reminding us of how lucky we were to be able to call her wife, mother, and friend.

Comments (A sampling)

Thanks Fred – this is wonderful. I had already resolved to take better care of myself physically, now I am resolved to be more tolerant and giving. WWTD – great! — Lin M.

So very beautifully said! That outpouring of gratitude for all Theresa's goodness will surely keep her light shining in our hearts and lives. Like the WWTD as a reminder. Theresa always expected Joy to prevail and would want us to honor her by living our lives that way. — Kate C.

Hello Fred, Such sadness, this loss of Theresa. Your heart hurts, as is to be expected, and I hope you take good care of yourself during the coming days and weeks. One of my favorite quotes about the passing of a loved one is from a 4th Century Bishop: "She whom we love and lose is no longer where she was before. She is now wherever we are." May it be so for you. Warmest greetings. – Mims H.

Fred, your tribute was beautiful. Thank you for sharing. I did share your post with a few people at LPL. This is a beautiful tribute to such an amazing and kind person. This news makes me so sad and humbles me at the same time. Life is way too short and precious to take for granted. May she have eternal peace, and officially become the angel she already was. God Bless. — Michelle P.

- ## Accepting Help and Including Others

I was also blessed to have the help of a sister and close friends to reduce the burden on me and my daughters. We were fortunate in that my wife had built a circle of twenty close friends, who combined with the neighbors, provided us with meals for nearly six weeks and paid for a full house cleaning after my wife passed. We received hundreds of cards and emails, which my daughters read to Theresa every day until she passed. She loved hearing and seeing them, as they gave her assurances of how much she was loved and supported during this transition. We mounted them on the fireplace and walls around her, so she could see them from her bed.

At a minimum, try to allow everyone to help who wants to contribute food and supplies. Again, if you are fortunate, as we were, there may be one or two friends who are willing to take charge of scheduling everyone else for food deliveries, so you are not trying to do this task too. Your ability to manage such tasks will be greatly diminished during this period.

Some close friends offered specific help, such as paying for a floral arrangement for our "Celebration of Life." If it fits with your needs, I urge you to accept these offers of help as they will greatly reduce the stress on you and your family. And do not get picky about how they help you. That is just a self-made distraction which serves no purpose.

As mentioned earlier, *you must take care of yourself physically, mentally, and emotionally.* This improved my ability to support my family as I was rested, felt relatively good physically, and I was not in a constant state of distress. I should warn you, that while this helps, it only goes so far. More later about the other stressors you will now find to be in your life.

• Continuing as Father and New Role as Ma/Grandma

One of the most difficult tasks for me as a father was to continue to honor and fulfill this role. My children were just as fearful, sad, upset, and discombobulated as I was--and they continued to look to me for cues, love and support.

While I needed to grieve, I also needed to openly share my feelings with my children and my grandchildren. I needed to continue providing strength and direction for our family. I included my daughters in every decision. They wanted to be a part of it. It made their role meaningful, their input was valued, and their ability to provide real support was encouraged.

Upon the death of my spouse, there was a huge void that could not be filled by anyone else. My children and grandchildren each had to process grief in their own personal way and pace. I had to resist the urge to tell them how to grieve; and allow each a private space. I would encourage them to participate in counseling at the local hospice. It was hard, but I made sure that I was there for them and willing to talk (yes, really talk) about:

- what had happened, how this was affecting all of us;
- what I expected of the unfolding experience moving forward;
- how much we needed each other's support and how we could support each other;
- where we all could turn for help (emotional, financial, counselling and so on); and,
- avoiding major decisions during the next few months until our mental state could become more normalized.

Besides watching me for signs of instability, they were looking at me to help fill that gap for them in spiritual, emotional, human, and practical ways. This included being more empathetic towards them, filling in for Grandma on shopping trips, helping with babysitting, buying meals for all where possible, taking the grandkids to their activities, talking to them more often to let them know that you are thinking of them, remembering birthdays, and being there for them during their special moments.

There is no way I could make up for everything Grandma did for them; they and I had to accept that! But I could help to soften the blow and fill a bit of their need for the love they were so desperately missing.

My grandchildren needed this attention, especially as they had a special bond to their grandmother. I discussed this with my children, and then asked them to let me know what I could do to help them and the grandkids.

One thing I did to help my children and grandchildren, through the initial grieving process was to give each one a love letter, that is, a handmade card with a note inside, from grandma, with a photo of her enclosed. This gesture helped me a great deal, too. My wife and I discussed this before her passing. She had been unable to do the cards herself, but she was so grateful for my suggestion and knew the kids and grandkids would appreciate them.

I knew exactly what she would want to say to each one of them, so it was easy to write the cards, which I started with, "Grandma asked me to write this special message to you because she loved you so much." After the opening line, I mentioned things that were special and unique about each child as well as how much she loved and appreciated each one. I enjoyed writing each one and felt my wife's presence as I prepared them. Right down to my very soul, I felt the connection these notes helped to forge between Theresa's heart and theirs.

These love letters are but one way to convey your wife's love for your children and grandchildren. I recommend you find a way that is uniquely yours or your wife's and then personalize it in your own way. The love letters can be particularly effective: Steal this idea freely! Look for unique materials, packaging, words, and symbols that say "mom" and "grandma" loud and clear. For me the love letters were written on personal greeting cards my wife had made. You will find little projects such as this are especially therapeutic for you as well.

- ## Taking Time to Grieve

Speaking from personal experience, I think that ideally you should stay out of the workplace for three months or more. The absolute minimum should be the first month, which is pure hell. I kept much of my emotional responses contained within the privacy of my home, as we men are well trained to not express ourselves in public.

At the very least, share with your employer—or your employees if you are an entrepreneur—that your responses and other behaviors may not be consistent with what they were before the death of your spouse.

Like me, you may experience many or all of the following:

- Real and strong physical pain, I had no idea one could hurt so much. It can permeate your gut and then whole body, crippling you at times for up to three or more days after her passing.
- Crying and sobbing spells
- The need to scream loudly to let your anger and frustration out
- Loss of sleep (I was lucky to get two hours many nights)
- Occasional surreal and hallucinatory type experiences
- Loss of emotional control, where every emotional reaction is multiplied times ten
- Anger (a single thoughtless comment can set you off)
- Inability to concentrate on anything but the most mundane tasks
- Depression and a desire to join your spouse
- A sense of your inability to survive this experience
- A constant need to tell your story repeatedly to everyone you meet (it is therapeutic)
- Frustration that you cannot see her in your mind or dreams (this may occur for months or years)

These can and probably will disrupt your ability to do your job at all, much less do it well. If you return to work too soon you may miss important opportunities to take on and complete therapeutic tasks which can be great ways to say goodbye to your spouse while grieving.

My big project was to clean and organize my wife's hobby room, a two-month project which brought me great comfort. Each card reflected her artistic sense, and every saying on every card was her personalized message to me and the world. One widower said the best thing that happened to him was that his basement flooded. It took him two months to clean it up. This critical task turned his attention away from his grieving for a time.

One struggle was that I quickly realized my wife was not in the things—clothing, bedding, jewelry, purses, shoes, belts, pillows, or any other items that she owned or used. It was frustrating because I could not feel her in much of anything anymore. I realized that she was really and forever gone. In no way did using these items of day-to-day life help me, such as wearing her robe, hugging her pillow, or laying on top of her clothes. The only items that I found helpful at all were the photos of her and the cards that she made. Your experience may be different, as it often is for every widow and widower.

For another therapeutic project, I spent over two months sorting, reviewing, and digitizing all our old photos. Each one I found was a small triumph, bringing back specific memories and helping me to achieve some closure.

I admit that I spoke to her each time I found a new photographic memory, and still do speak to her every day. Since I now had no one at home to speak to every morning and night, speaking out loud was one way to cope with her absence. Because we had lived together for years on end, I pretty much knew what her response would be as well.

If you do not take the time to grieve, many studies show that you risk a full-blown melt-down in the future, very possibly at a most un-expected moment. It is better to confront the grief head on, challenge it, and work your way through it so you can move forward with your life once you are ready to do so. If you put off the grieving process you may have the added guilt of not having grieved earlier.

If the dying process was over an extended period, such as over a year or more, you may have already been experiencing many of the grieving symptoms as you dealt with the reality and the inevitability of her impending death. A neighbor of mine was back to work a week af-ter her husband passed from a two-year brain tumor that caused him to steadily deteriorate.

In these cases, your post-death grieving process may be considera-bly shorter than what is considered within the normal range. And the reality is that many experts on this process will assert that the grieving process is unique to every person, so don't obsess about whether yours is too long, too short, too painful, or not painful enough.

- ## Celebration of Life/Funeral Service

I had a choice upon the loss of my wife. Either I could go into full isolation mode and not deal with anyone about anything having to do with her death, or I could focus and deal first with things like "Closure" events, such as a funeral or "celebration of life" gathering.

With my daughters' support we decided to do a "Celebration of Life" event at a nearby restaurant, to which we invited all our families, friends, and neighbors. It was therapeutic even though we were all still in a state of shock. I disengaged emotionally as I sleep-walked through the event, knowing why I was there and that she was gone, but not really knowing what the heck that meant. I exchanged thankyous for each condolence, hugging lots of guests, and trying to honor and celebrate her life with those who cared for her.

While my children and I were the centerpiece of the event, we had to remember that all our guests were suffering the loss too. They loved and cared for her as we did, and they wanted to say goodbye in a way which was respectful and in keeping with her personality and style. They wanted to let me, and my family know that they cared.

I believe it is much better to do one big event than to have all those people calling and coming over to your house one at a time. I just could not handle that kind of intrusion into my life during the grieving period. When you are home you really want to be left alone to grieve privately.

So, I hate to say it, but I just had to put on a brave face, get through the event, and then afterwards allow myself to fully enter the grieving mode. My self-protective ego system helped me to do what I thought I could not do, and to do it with courage and strength, and without breaking down out of control while doing it. Somehow, I made it through it, and then…the full blast uninterrupted grieving started.

The following Caring Bridge entries are an example of how we took advantage or the web site to announce the Celebration of Life, to document it, and then to share it out with everyone.

Caring Bridge #11: Celebration of Life
by Charlene Olms, July 3, 2015

Hello friends. Many of you have been asking about our plans for funeral arrangements. With Theresa's blessing, we have planned for a Celebration of Life. As you all know, she was not very big on being the center of attention and never wanted a large funeral at which we would all be wallowing. However, she was open to a small informal gathering.

We apologize that we were not able to extend an invitation to everyone (as many are out of state), but instead asked family and those area friends that were closest to her to attend. The event will take place at Wahoo's, a casual restaurant where she loved to treat the family to meals complete with giggling and rambunctious grandchildren.

There will be a taco bar, because she loved her Mexican food. There will be lovely photos on display and lots of reminiscing of good times. We will post photos afterwards. In lieu of flowers, please consider sending a donation in honor of Theresa to Pathways Hospice. If you would like to discuss more personal options for the family, feel free to contact Charlene at her email address. Thank you all for your love and support. Charlene O.

Caring Bridge #12: Celebration of Life
by Charlene Olms, July 7, 2015

On July 6, many friends and family members gathered to honor Theresa.

Her Celebration of Life was held at Wahoo's Restaurant. It was a perfect setting for a casual gathering in which loving memories were shared. Dad, Jennifer and I appreciated all those who could make it and all those who were there in spirit. Mom would have adored seeing all those loving faces in one place, but she would have certainly been embarrassed that it was all about her and what an AMAZING person she was.

With love, Charlene

- ## Post Celebration – What now?

Try to block off considerable time after the "Celebration of Life" or funeral service to allow unfettered grieving. This could be weeks, or it could be months.

Even if your spouse had a long-term illness prior to her death, the finality of her passing hits you hard. There is no longer a thread of hope, you now know she will never return.

If you have completed some of the grieving process before her passing, you are likely to still need time to adjust to your new reality as a widower.

I awoke to the realization that I was now alone, and I no longer had the day-to-day duties of caring for her. I found that a big hole opened in my heart and my day. I had to find the right way to say my goodbyes —a lengthy and painful process that can continue for months if not years—and to survive the days to come.

At the time, I thought this post would be my final Caring Bridge entry. I quickly found I had much more to write and share with friends and family, eventually writing more than thirty posts/blogs over the next year. We each need to find a vehicle through which we can say and share our grief. This process is therapeutic and helps you process your grief.

Caring Bridge #13: Final Goodbye to Theresa
by Fred Colby, July 8, 2015

While many of us will continue to say goodbye to our beautiful and generous Theresa in our own way over the coming weeks, months, and even years... It is time for us to say our final goodbyes on Caring Bridge.

We are grateful to have found this great web site, so we could be in constant communication with so many of you during this time of trial. Through this vehicle, we could connect with many old friends who might otherwise have been left out of the loop. Theresa, I, and our two great daughters were very appreciative of every word of support and encouragement.

Theresa heard every comment that came in before her passing, and you could just see her eyes well up with gratitude for every one of them. It gave her the knowledge that she was much loved and the strength to see things through at the end. I know she was at peace in part because she had been able to connect with all of you, and because she knew your prayers and love would carry her forward.

Jennifer, Charlene, Robert (Theresa's brother), and I will never be able to thank you all enough for all your support. It made it all a little more bearable. We thank you and look forward to seeing and speaking with all of you again in the future.

Gratefully, Fred, Jennifer, Charlene, and Robert

Comments (A sampling)

Yes, this was a wonderful way to get updates and communicate with Theresa and her family, without imposing during this emotional time. She touched so many lives, and we are all grieving. Thank you for helping us with that. The pictures were wonderful to have also. Love you all. Linnie — Lin M.

The grace you showed by taking the time to communicate with everyone helped us all get through our dear Theresa's passing as well. Not being close enough to see you all and give you the hugs and other support would have been unbearable, but for your willingness to include those of us who are far away! Again, you have set a most wonderful example! Thank you so very much! — Rita H.

- ## Avoiding Major Decisions for a Year

You may often hear the advice to avoid making any major decisions for at least a year after your wife's passing. In general, I have found this to be true, not only for myself, but also for the many widowers and widows I have met since my loss. At minimum, the decisions one should avoid include remarrying, selling your house and moving, and giving away all your wife's possessions. They may also include job changes and complete life style changes. Yet, some may find themselves in circumstances that dictate these changes.

I found my life was about to change in a big way, and I would be thrust into new activities, new relationships, and new ways of thinking that would have a major impact upon my future. To get through it all, I needed to keep some stability in my life, such as home, family, and friends. All I could do to prepare for these changes was to be aware, and to be willing to stop and seriously consider consequences before making significant changes in my life. This approach helped me to avoid some of the major pitfalls that some other widowers who I know experienced.

In *Widower: When Men are Left Alone*, authors Scott Campbell and Phyllis Silverman quote a contributor as saying,

I did absolutely positively the worst thing you could do. I gave away all her clothes in two weeks. I sold the house very quickly and moved. I packed up and moved to Santa Barbara, just two months after she died, so I could be near my son . . . When I got here, I was very depressed. I had actually quit eating and didn't even know it. I had lost more than seventy pounds . . . I decided to kill myself . . . See, I literally had no friends.[1]

The contributor, named Roger, did eventually get his life back together with the assistance of volunteers, counselors, and peers through Widowed Persons Services. He eventually went through training, so he could help others. You will find that helping others is one way to deal with your grief in a therapeutic and positive way which benefits your healing process.

Chapter 4

Coping with Grief

The depth of your love for your wife, will either drive you to run as fast as you can away from grieving or it will force you to confront the grief head on. The latter can be an attempt to employ the grief as a way to honor and remember your wife. She is gone. But everything she instilled in you through your life together, including core values, are still there to support and guide you.

Some of the best advice I got during the early days of my grieving process was to "embrace the grief" and don't fight it. I learned to look at the grieving process as an opportunity to remember, honor, and love the one I lost. Each pang of suffering was a reminder of how special Theresa was to me. It allowed me to connect with my wife in a way that cannot be replicated through other means. As bad as it was, I pretty much had to just accept it and work my way through it.

Alan Wolfelt, Ph.D. of the Center for Loss & Life Transition, advises,

> Express your grief openly. When you share your grief outside yourself, healing occurs. Allow yourself to talk about the circumstances of the death, your feelings of loss and loneliness, and the special things you miss about your spouse . . . Whatever you do, don't ignore your grief . . . Allow yourself to speak from your heart, not just from your head . . . It takes a great deal of energy and effort to heal.[2]

Grief unfolds over time in a way which is unique to each person. Like me, you may feel there is something wrong with you, and become afraid of being embarrassed or of looking crazy in front of friends or family. This is a normal reaction and I found that I could work my way past this fear over time. I learned to not be self-condemning and to be patient with myself.

If your wife experienced a long and painful period prior to her passing, you may have processed some grief prior to her death. One widower who experienced this said,

> The main part of my grieving was actually done before she died. I'd call it anticipatory grief. . . Here, you come thinking on what it will be like to live alone, what you will do, what you'll have to learn . . . If you pretend, if you try to ignore . . . I think that is a bad thing to do. You're not going to postpone death . . . In a sense, I was glad she died. At least she was relieved of her pain.[3]

Following is a brief outline of the Dual Process of Grief, an accepted way of viewing the grief process. I also include a brief review of the "Five Stages of Grief," an often referred to model by Elisabeth Kubler-Ross, but now a somewhat less prevalent view of the grief process.

1. **Dual Process of Grief**: The Dual Process Model of Grief is a very helpful process first described by Margaret Stroebe and Henk Schut of Utrecht University in The Netherlands in a 2010 paper entitled "The Dual Process Model of Coping with Bereavement: A Decade On."

    They state that most people will experience normal grief by seesawing between loss-oriented and restoration-oriented responses.

    The Stroebe-Shut model captures why many people feel as though they are on an emotional roller coaster that includes *loss-oriented responses*—grieving, crying, the desire to hide from the world — and *restoration-oriented responses*— pursuing new challenges, forming new relationships. During the latter, the grieving person is able to focus on day-to-day tasks and get some relief from the emotional drain of the loss of his loved one.

    Grief hits on multiple levels— physical, emotional, psychological, and spiritual. It's normal to feel distracted, tired, agitated, forgetful, and even short tempered. You might also have pains, such as a headache or stomach ache, and sigh deeply with no real provocation.

The authors of the Dual Process Model note that about 10 percent of bereaved people will experience Complicated Grief; if that occurs a licensed grief therapist can help. Complicated grief involves intense, long-term, debilitating experience of loss. If you feel you fall into this category, find a grief counselor or therapist. Most people never know that, however; they simply move back and forth in the Dual Process of Grief in a normal way.

By giving yourself permission to experience both styles of coping, you will contribute to your emotional balance, and work through your loss in a healthy way.

Mindfulness practices like meditation and yoga can help, too. If you experience intense emotion, breathe slowly and deeply to anchor and calm yourself.

Ruth Davis Konigsberg reported in Association for the Advancement of Retired Persons (AARP) magazine on the "5 Surprising Truths About Grief" that, "We don't grieve in stages at all, but oscillate rapidly. Over time those swings diminish in both frequency and intensity until we reach a level of emotional adjustment."[4]

This has been for the most part true in my experience, except for one major exception! Even after I reached a sort of stabilization, I could still be blindsided by a sudden emotional response that took me down to the depths again. I have heard this frequently from widows and widowers.

But, acute grief (what I refer to as the deep grieving cycle) is not a permanent state. The same article cited George A. Bonanno, a clinical psychologist at Columbia University, as having found that the core symptoms of grief, including anxiety, shock, depression, and intrusive thoughts, had dissipated six months after the loss for half of the participants. Some people took up to eighteen months or even three years to resume normal functioning. Bonanno's conclusion was that, while loss is forever, acute grief is not.[5]

2. **Five Stages of Grief**: Many publications still list the standards developed by Dr. Kubler-Ross. It. includes:
   a) Denial – earliest stage where you become numb and deny the loss ever happened

b) Anger – you will likely express anger at all sorts of causes of loss, including God, doctors, and others
c) Bargaining – you will do anything to spare your spouse this fate, to save her, to get her back, to return to normal
d) Depression – withdrawing from life and entering a period of great sadness
e) Acceptance – the point when you accept the reality of her passing

These stages are covered in some depth in materials at the library and bookstore and available at your local hospice. Well regarded experts advise that you not get locked in to thinking that your grief must follow these five areas, much less follow them in any specific order or for specific time frames. Each person's experience is unique and may differ significantly from the model in the process.

Heather Stang notes in a 2014 article titled "5 Stages of Grief: Are They Real?" that there is a problem with relying on the Five Stages of Grief, "these are observations of the dying patient, not those left behind to grieve. In fact, there has been no research project to date that has been able to prove that the 5 Stages of Grief are universal."[1] However, as recently as July of 2016 a major publication, *Psychotherapy Networker*, published an article titled "Moving Through Grief" by David Kessler that extolled the benefits of using the Kubler-Ross model.

Many do observe that anger is uniquely strong for men. Men often seek outlets for their anger, ranging from breaking a set of dishes, chopping wood, taking it out on a punching bag, or throwing things until their anger is spent and they can allow the other aspects of grief to take over. However, this is not always true.

I did have some anger prior to my wife's death (which I took out on the local Home Owners Association). I did not have any deep anger moments after her death. That does not mean that I did not yell, scream, and punch a few things. I did. But this was short-lived in most cases, with only the yelling and screaming continuing.

Other Views of Grief: I found several publications aimed towards men in grief that recommend that you face your demons, and not hide from them as this only allows them to grow stronger. You must stand up to them until you defeat them. (See *Swallowed by a Snake: The Gift* *of the Masculine Side of Healing*, by Thomas R. Golden, 1996).

Swallowed by a Snake emphasized that grief is not a sign of weakness. In fact, in many cultures men openly embrace the grief in male oriented rituals and customs such as shooting arrows into the sky or gathering with other men in dances expressing their sorrow and anger. One example cited in the book was how one man upon finding out about his spouse's death, went outside with other men at a gathering and had them hold him down while he let out his anger and sorrow physically and verbally.

Pathways in Fort Collins, Colorado explains The Grief Experience using a Grief Wheel which divides the experience into five categories:

1. **Feelings** such as guilt, sadness, shock, fear, relief, panic, loneliness, anxiety, fatigue, numbness, regret, anger and yearning

2. **Thought Processes** such as suicidal thoughts, hallucinations, sense of presence of your wife, preoccupation, disbelief, and confusion

3. **Physical Sensations** such as headaches, lack of energy, dry mouth, heart palpitations, noise sensitivity, appetite increase or decrease, nausea or upset stomach, weakness, breathlessness, chest tightness

4. **Spiritual** Exercises such as religious rituals, asking Who am I? questioning your values and beliefs., What is my purpose? Is there a God? Is there afterlife? Why?

5. **Behaviors** such as treasuring spouse's possessions, self-destructive behaviors (alcohol and drugs, relationships), sleep disturbances, appetite changes, calling for spouse, over-activity, withdrawal, dreams of deceased, lethargy, crying, and sighing.

I identified various times during my grief when I experienced each of these categories. In summary, all the current and past models of the grief experience provide some value in your effort to understand what you are going through and what you can expect going forward.

The following sections are drawn from my own experiences, often validated through conversations with other widowers and research.

- ## Physical Pain

Nothing could prepare me for the first waves of physical pain that I experienced the first few days after my wife's passing. It literally doubled me over and forced me to the floor the first three to five days. It was not constant, but it was frequent and overwhelming.

I could not breathe at first; my stomach felt like someone had punched it repeatedly. For a while, I did not know how a person could survive this pain. And while it was happening I did not know when, if ever, it would end. I was so deeply immersed in my grief that each symptom seemed like it would go on forever.

This was combined with crying, sobbing, screaming, and other symptoms. It was suspended during the times I was out doing things I could not escape doing, such as the funeral/cremation arrangements, but would return full force when I was home alone again.

I cannot suggest any solution, medication, or activities that will diminish the impact of this pain; just know that you can and will get through it. The only alternative is to become engaged in outside distractions that prevent you from experiencing this area of grief, but my own suspicion is that will only delay the event. Escaping grief may even amplify your grieving, as well as introduce guilt into your collection of regrets for things not done.

- ## Crying and Sobbing – Dry Heaves of Crying

While this probably will vary from man to man, I found myself wracked by a form of crying and sobbing which consisted of gasping for air while sobbing full throttle, but without all that many tears. To me it compared to the dry heaves as you are gasping for air when trying to throw up, but you cannot. I experienced this often during the first month. Eventually I learned to just give into it and let it run its course. As with some of the other symptoms you will find that these "crying" bouts will strike most ferociously when you are home alone (thank God). It usually happens when you know you can let it out privately.

My stress and lack of sleep during this period led to delusions and failed memories. For some widowers, their perceived reality becomes distorted. In *Widower: When Men are Left Alone*, one interviewee misremembered his first six months of grieving as a period of inactivity. He felt he was so preoccupied by the loss of his wife that he was virtually paralyzed, except to cry and feel sad. When he later shared that with his mother, she corrected him, reminding him that he had been on the road quite a bit with his job. When he looked at his mileage log, he found—much to his surprise, that she was right.

Men, per other publications I could find on this topic, do cry much less than women during this grieving period. I think this deep-seated resistance by men to crying is why I experienced the dry heave sobbing version. I could not just let the tears flow, so this weird form of sobbing took over.

In *Crying: The Mystery of Tears*, author William Frey notes that men cry less in part due to physiological reasons, less prolactin, which is a hormone instrumental to tear production. This makes it difficult for men to connect with their bodies while in grief.

When out in public, with friends or with family, my crying would usually be limited to a few tears or glassy eyes. Men naturally "tough it out" and resist the full throttle crying that our female counterparts can often yield to so readily. At first you may ask, "What is wrong with me? Why can I not cry for my wife?" Don't condemn yourself for this lack of crying. It is what we are, and you just learn to go with the flow and know that you are grieving properly for her, and if possible, she knows it too.

Thomas R. Golden, LCSW, explains in *The Way Men Heal* that testosterone plays a role in crying. The hormone subdues our crying response to an emotional situation and diminishes our ability to express emotions verbally while feeling them.

There are cultures where the men grieve much more openly. Even there, however, these men grieve much differently and often through rituals which express anger as a key component of the process (for example, shooting arrows into the sky). I believe that you should not get hung up on differences between how you grieve and how others are said to grieve.

If there is one thing I learned repeatedly while going through this process, it is that each of us is unique in how we grieve. There is no wrong way and no right way.

• Craving for Wife's Embrace and Lovemaking

Don't be surprised if shortly after your wife's passing you have a strong physical need to embrace your wife and make love to her, though she is not present. This can include normal sexual responses. Based on my experience, and conversations with other widowers, this can occur as early as the day after her passing to within a very few days or weeks. For others, it may never happen.

Like me, you may arrive at the point where you would gladly be with just about any woman to regain that feeling of physical contact and the act of making love. I believed this was needed to feel less abandoned, and less lost in the painful void I found myself in all the time. However, the alternative of falling in bed with the first willing or a paid woman would have opened me up to a whole series of possible repercussions, including a sense of betrayal, regret, and self-doubt. It just was not in my DNA, although I know of others who did give into these urges.

Becoming involved with a new woman too soon after your wife's passing can lead to irreparable harm to you and your loved ones. We are so desperate for companionship that we can become blinded to the obvious problems with the relationship. You need to first process your grief and recognize your new reality before trying to fill the void left by your wife's departure.

Other widowers who have spoken to me or participated in interviews in *Widower: When Men are Left Alone*, indicate that acting on this desperate need can be a common experience. When one does act on these urges, the next challenge may be to avoid falling into a cycle of self-condemnation.

Having survived this phase without acting on these various urges, I recommend, Don't give into these urges. You will survive this!

Based on my own experience and research, masturbation is a very normal outlet for this craving. Your wife is the one you are most likely to be fantasizing about making love with at these times. Though my physical desire was overwhelming at times, I realized that physically replacing my wife with another woman would not replace her mentally, emotionally, or spiritually.

> **Alternate Reality**: I caution you that impotence can
> also be a common experience after a wife passes, so
> don't presume that something is wrong with you if
> this is your reaction.

After my experience, and what I saw and heard from other widowers, I believe the hyper-emotional state during the deep grieving period,
which lasts for 4 – 6 months at minimum, makes good decisions about
relationships to be near impossible.

Widower: When Men are Left Alone documents cases in which men
either remarried too fast or had an intimate relationship too soon after
their wife's passing. Remarrying too soon can be hazardous, with the
widower putting "another bridal doll on top of the cake" so he can continue with his life. These marriages often fail with both parties hurt
badly. I have met many widows who avoided entering a new meaningful relationship for years after their husband died. In contrast, almost
every widower I have met has entered a new relationship within
months, if not within a year, of their wife's passing.

One widower I know avoided counselors and processing of his
grief with others until he entered a relationship a few months after his
loss. Months later that relationship broke up, yet another upset that he
had great difficulty accepting. This eventually led to him having to face
some of the grieving issues he had avoided up to that point.

The results were just as traumatic for him, maybe worse, as they
would have been much earlier in his grieving.

If you feel ready, as I did, you might start dating before six months
after death, but I recommend being on guard about taking these relationships to the intimate stage for at least a month or two if you can.
Every month delayed will help you to enter an intimate stage in a
healthier place. I can testify that once you get to a healthier place your
new relationship can be everything you hope for and more.

If too early, I found that I would think that I had control and would
be overcome with euphoria and anxiety at alternate times (part of the
hyper-emotional response). I did not have things under control. It was
months before I saw how out of control I was during this period. It is
fair to warn you there are as many needy women as there are men, and
they may take advantage of your vulnerability if you are not careful.

I dated one woman starting in my fifth month after becoming a widower. She was two years removed from losing her husband. We both were way too hyper-emotional and not ready for an intimate relationship. The ups and downs, the drama, and the uncertainty about what we really wanted doomed the relationship from the start. But, it was a good learning experience for both of us.

One year later, I was grateful that we had not entered a sexual relationship. I came to discover later all the reasons why we would not have made good long-term partners.

For your own sanity and the ability to come out of the grieving with your other relationships (family, friends, employment, church family) still intact, remember the quality of your new relationship is more important than the speed with which you satisfy your physical desires.

As men, we have few opportunities to touch women without sexual connotations being implied. So, when we crave the touch of a woman, our psycho-emotional response is to crave sex, as this is at the core of our beliefs. It happens without aforethought, and you have little or no control over it when it happens. I was so over the top emotionally, that self-control was limited, and my usual boundaries no longer applied.

I was blessed to have women friends who were willing to hug, touch, or provide shoulder rubs without it having sexual overtones. I was grateful and often took advantage of this as it helped to reduce the cravings as well.

One trick is to constantly be on the alert to your mind presuming that every touch has sexual overtones when it does not. Be on guard and ready to deny those thoughts any hold over you. (I love a Billy Bob Thornton skit on *Big Bang Theory* where every time a woman touched him he would say "One Mississippi, Two Mississippi, Three Mississippi." If he made it to the last one, he presumed she was into him and ready for him to make overtures towards her).

I found this craving to diminish over time from the strong overwhelming feelings that I had during the first few days and weeks after her passing. If you know it is not going to continue at that level it may be easier to get through it. You might feel guilty about fantasizing about other women, and you may continue to imagine your wife is still there with you until you begin to emerge from the grief cycles and turn your attention to seeing other women again—a whole different topic.

I want to emphasize that each of us will have a unique experience and each must discover what our emotional and biological needs are. I have met widowers who became impotent for a period of time, while others—myself included—felt like we were entering the rutting season much like the elk in Estes Park, Colorado. Just know that whatever your physiological reaction, you will eventually emerge from it and begin to achieve normalcy again.

• Shutting Others Out

For men, shutting out your friends and family is often preferred over facing one's emotions, confronting one's anger, and appearing vulnerable in front of those you most-rely upon for respect and self-image. A painful, but valuable discovery, for me and many other men, is that to be vulnerable in front of others is a sign of strength. Think about it, how often has someone confided something that made him vulnerable with you? And how often did you think that took courage to do, rather than thinking he was weak for sharing it?

If I don't tell my family and friends when I need help, who is going to tell them? If I hide in my home or behind a façade of stoic independent strength, how would I heal? My strategy, which turned out to be effective, was to be open with everyone, not only through my blogs, but also in one-on-one meetings.

I found that if you have a circle of friends, even if it is primarily through your wife, they will be looking for indicators from you that you are welcoming of opportunities to get together, to go out places, to join them for dinner, and so on. If I had not sent signals they would likely have stayed away thinking that I wanted space and time away from everyone.

I had to work on maintaining my friendships by reaching out to them and letting them know how they could support me. If I had not, many would have disappeared over time. Some friends will try to help you, at least until they feel that you do not want them to. Only a few friends will stick with it if you are not responsive.

Each person is different, it may take weeks or months before you are comfortable going out with others. Or, you might feel like a third wheel with married friends and prefer to only go out with the "guys."

As you will see in some of the following, I used blogs to let friends and family know that I was fine with getting together, but, that they in turn should be okay with my tearing up over remembering my wife. I also let them know that I did want to talk about it, and not try to ignore the elephant in the room.

My friends and family were very responsive to this and they often invited me out for coffee, lunch, a beer, and even dinner at their house. Each visit allowed me to make progress in my journey to becoming a part of our community again, to being able to engage in normal relationships again, and to prepare for once again being fully functional.

It was not easy, and there were times when I wanted to retreat to my safe house again. But, in keeping with the "confront my demons" strategy, I found that getting out was the best way to work my way through the various stages or symptoms of grief.

> **Alternate Reality:** Some "friends" will not be able to handle the real and hyper-emotional you during this period. Some will fall by the wayside forever, and some for a period. Like me, you may have to learn to just accept that and let them go. They are not the ones you need in your life right now. I found that what I needed are those who are loyal friends, those who stuck by me regardless of my state of mind.

The following Caring Bridge entries demonstrate some of my grief processing and how I was reaching out to others to help me through it. Comments from friends and family can show how others valued your wife and honor her. This offers valuable support for you at this time.

Caring Bridge #14: One Month After
by Fred Colby, July 30, 2015

It has been a tough month to say the least. One saving grace is all the great photos I have of Theresa. The one posted here as the main photo is by far my favorite. It captures Theresa's pure joy, her impishness, and just plain fun. We had many opportunities to dance during my years in the arts, fundraising for nonprofits, and community events.

We fit together well, and we enjoyed each other's company at such events... and you know Theresa, she loved people watching while there.

During our many years together, we met a lot of interesting people, and she made the most of it. No hesitation on her part, she would go right up to them and get her picture if possible no matter what...she just had fun... which of course made my life a whole lot more enjoyable too.

Comments (A sampling)

Not, everyone is blessed enough to be in love and stay in love for so many years... you both are an inspiration. — ANA B.

I remember going to functions with Theresa when Fred couldn't go. One time she'd be "Frank" next time I'd be "Frank." Once at Fred's mom's, at an art show, Ted Geisel was there. She was so excited. I had no idea who he was till she said he was Dr. Seuss. — Mary R.

She was one of the most fun people I've ever known, always making every situation enjoyable, even when some would grumble! She always saw the best in others! No wonder we love her so much!!! —Rita H.

Caring Bridge #15: Theresa and Family
by Fred Colby, August 3, 2015

I love this photo as it shows Theresa (and me too) at our best as young parents growing into our roles. Theresa is clearly no longer a young girl bride in this photo, she is beautiful and there is a touch of sophistication and confidence about her that came out as she matured.

It was a fun and exciting time with the girls growing up, Theresa in full mom mode with lots of area friends and activities, and me joining the San Diego Community College Board. As Theresa grew in self-confidence and built her relationships she only became stronger and more fun. We are all missing her, but the memories are wonderful.

- **Trip to Temporary Solitude & Its Benefits**

Solitude is an inactive mode and a potent healer. Often grieving men will gravitate towards solitude.
Thomas R. Golden, *The Way Men Heal*

Following our Celebration of Life, I immediately left for a five-day solo escape to a mountain cabin where I could fully engage with my grief uninterrupted. There was no cell signal, no television, one radio station, and nobody to interfere with my process. The first two days were living Hell, with a capital "H." For the first time, I confronted the fact that she was gone forever, that I would never hold her again, never speak to her again, and never engage with her in any way again.

I could scream and sob and cry as much as I wanted without fear that I would cause concern for others such as my neighbors, friends, and family. They knew why I went, and pretty much left me alone other than an occasional check in call on the land line phone.

The third through fifth days in solitude were still very rough and painful, but I was able to achieve an equilibrium point at which I could express my grief vocally and emotionally while gaining gradual control over it. I still cried, yelled, and wondered if this was a surreal unreality from which I would emerge at some point. I could begin to see that I could and would survive this—in part, because I knew I had to!

I had to, so I could support my kids and grandkids through what was to come, so I could settle all the estate issues that would come up, and so I could provide a model of strength for everyone close to me, so they could survive it too. I knew that as the patriarch of the family, quitting was not an option! And if I could not quit, then I knew I had to work my way through all of this, so my kids and grandkids could survive whole and hopefully undamaged by the experience.

Other widowers who see themselves as the "protector/provider" may often be unwilling or even incapable of showing their grief with others around. They can be afraid to reveal their vulnerability, to cry in front of others, to appear weak. And in many cases their fears may be well-founded, as children and others may react with concern and even fear when they see their dad breaking down emotionally and physically.

I needed to get this grief expressed and processed. If I did not, I saw firsthand how it could build up and come out in a way which would trouble me more than even the grief itself. Thus, the need for a period of solitude if you can in any way arrange for it. While my choice was a mountain cabin, a beach bungalow separated from others will do just as well. Imagine your scream at its loudest, and that will give you an idea of why you need some space between you and neighbors.

While I do believe that talking about what you are going through can be very helpful, I found that there are times during the early deep grieving process that I just needed to be able to vent all my anger and frustration without worrying about others. Getting away is one way to process some of this most poignant and painful grief.

Something about being able to scream in the woods or on the beach is immensely therapeutic. I still needed to vent more of my anger and frustration after I returned home, but, I learned to contain most of this within the confines of my home.

What to Take with You: For me, I knew that I needed to understand better what I was facing as I entered this unknown grieving process. In addition to religious writings which I thought might be helpful, I also took materials I had printed from various web sites about the grieving process. Each day in the mountains I would review some of these insights, which gave me some confidence that what I was going through was normal, and that I could survive this.

I recommend taking this book or one like it, and maybe spiritually oriented materials that you feel comfortable with. I really did not feel like reading other books. Long walks and time to think and process are what is important. Everything else can wait.

I made a point of trying to regain an emotionally centered and positive basis for thinking about my wife and what I was going through. To help me accomplish this, I wrote a list of things I was grateful for in the life that I shared with my wife. Such as our first meeting, her faithfulness to me, her confidence in me, the trips we took together, her exceptional skills as a mom, her joy and liveliness, and personal things such as how she would scratch my head.

I also made a list of reasons why I should not grieve so much, including the fact that she would not want me to, the support I needed to provide the daughters and grandchildren, and because we had forty-five great years together for which I should be immensely grateful.

• Temptation of Alcohol and Drugs

Grief can introduce all kinds of life-threatening stressors and these can often trigger accompanying unhealthy old and new bad behaviors. Self-recrimination, self-doubts, questioning of your core self-image can lead to destructive behaviors.

As with any time when you are in a depressed state, the siren call of alcohol and drugs may be strong. I was very tempted to drink more than I usually did, to try some weed (something I had not had for 47 years), or to try some pain pills. All of this was to ease the pain and help to just forget about what I was going through at that time.

Unfortunately, I found that this led into even more depression, with my wallowing in sorrow and even sinking into suicidal thoughts. The few times I did allow myself that extra drink (especially when drinking at home by myself) the wallowing in sorrow took over. I no longer had any semblance of control over these thoughts.

The temptation to just go deeper and deeper into the depression is powerful and self-destructive. If you do have or did have problems in the past with addictive behaviors, it is even more critical that you avoid alcohol and drugs.

Once again, the thing that helped me most to avoid a repetition of this behavior was to remember my kids and grandkids. I knew this was not the behavior my wife would have wanted to see, and that my kids needed me as much if not more than ever before.

When out drinking with friends I kept my intake down to no more than two beers or glasses of wine and avoided the hard stuff altogether. I could enjoy myself with them but keep the reins on my grieving.

If you are having any problems in this area, this is another reason you should be talking to other people, whether it be a counselor, friend, grief groups, or members of a group such as Alcoholics Anonymous (AA). However, one widower I know found the AA groups no longer met his needs, even though they had before. The members were emotionally disconnected from his experience and he felt put off by them and their conversations. If this is the case, you might consider finding other types of groups of men or a couple of male friends or relatives that you can bond with and with whom you can talk openly with about your experience.

- ## Suicidal Thoughts, Fear of Death and Building Resilience

You may entertain thoughts of suicide. I know I did.

Let me start by saying the loss of your fear of death is not the same as being suicidal. Widows and widowers who I have spoken with have told me that they are no longer afraid of dying. The reasons can vary from their willingness to rejoin the deceased spouse, to the experience of watching a loved one dying, to a feeling of having lived their life to the fullest and not being worried about things left undone. I don't know how universal this is, only that for me and many of my acquaintances our experience has somehow changed our view of death in general.

I was fortunate in that I did not experience deep suicidal thoughts, but it is likely to cross your mind as you wonder if life is worth living without your lifelong companion. Depression is very much inescapable. Nonetheless, you can take steps to identify and confront suicidal feelings when they do occur. You may even feel ambushed by them—surrounded on all sides. Even that is normal.

I had to learn to process my grief, which inevitably took me into a phase of depression, which if allowed to run rampant, would harm my physical and mental health, and could lead to suicidal thoughts. Engaging with others, and meeting a counselor helped me confront and overcome these thoughts.

I had to learn to recognize the difference between depression and self-destructive thoughts. If you have these feelings and cannot expel them, I urge you speak with a counselor as soon as is possible. If not, at least find that friend or relative who you can be open with. Getting things off your chest and expressed can improve your ability to overcome depression.

One strategy was to focus on the good in my time with my wife (more on this later), on the love we shared, and on how lucky I had been to have her in my life. I would reinforce these good thoughts with gratitude to God for sharing her with me. And finally, a tried and true method for me was to think about what she would want! It was not likely that she would have wanted me to suffer more, much less commit suicide.

Based on my experience and that of other widowers I spoke with, escaping the grieving process through too-early relationships can cause a widower to enter an even more depressive cycle after that new relationship begins to break down. Anxiety is a normal part of any relationship. While in a heightened hyper-emotional state, anxiety can become overwhelming and dominate your thinking day and night.

When I was in the middle of one complicated relationship, I spent hours obsessing about it. Sleepless nights became the norm again, contributing to other symptoms, such as delusional thinking and suicidal thoughts. This can lead to further consequences in the relationship which feeds a cycle of self-destructive actions and feelings. Only as I put the self-induced anxiety out of mind did I regain my more stable mental state.

I had to be cognizant of the fact that I was desperately trying to replace my wife with the first nice woman I met, the first truly pleasant gal who tried to reciprocate and make me happy. This realization led me to conclude that if I moved too fast due to my desperation, that I would very possibly really hurt my new friend when it all inevitably came to an ignoble end. It is easy to lie to yourself, and to her, as you try to force an outcome driven by an emotionally distraught state of mind.

How to Rebuild Resilience While Reducing Suicidal Thoughts

As I learned to confront my own demons, to counter depressive feelings, and to cast out suicidal thoughts, I was also strengthening my resilience. That is how I was able to strengthen my ability to bounce back from the low points of my experience during the grieving process.

Paula Stephens writes in her web site crazygoodgrief.com about the need to rebuild our resilience muscles. The following is quoted from an email she sent out on the topic on April 17 of 2016.

"How to Bounce Back Better! By Paula Stephens

A concept which I'm fascinated with is that of "Resilience"—in other words, why do some people bounce back from adversity like rubber balls and others hit to bottom with no bounce?

When I am in communities of loss there is rarely a distinct pattern of how well someone has integrated their experience (bounced back) when they are 1 year out, 2 years out, 3 years, etc. We all know each journey is unique—BUT are there things we can be doing that support building our emotional bounce? Because if there is—I want to do them!

I believe that training and remolding our brain for positive traits like gratitude and resilience aren't that much different than training our body for a 5k. It takes focused "training" (on the right stuff—don't ride a bike, if you want to run better) and knowledge of what works best (run short and fast or long and slow?).

And here's the good news—Resilience CAN be learned, and it's not primarily driven by genetics. Which means even if you've never been resilient or you're a family of floppers not bouncers – you can still learn to build your resilience muscles!

5 Ways to Build Your Resilience

Here's what I found out about building resilience – it goes hand-in-hand with the ways I advocate that we integrate our loss into our life. The tips listed below are from an article in Experience Life Magazine.

1. **Pump Up Your Positivity:** Be the person who looks for the silver lining! Yes... feel the tough emotions, but not at the expense of not feeling the good ones too. As you've heard me say before - Learn to hold both JOY & SADNESS in the same moment.

2. **Live to Learn:** Years ago while struggling with my son Daniel I had a therapist say to me, *"Well, that's an AFGO!"* Naturally I had no idea what he was talking about. So he explained - *Another F^&*ing Growth Opportunity.* Shift your focus to questioning what you can learn or what the various options are. Then stay away from questions that invite the blame game.

3. **Open Your Heart:** Love this one! It makes me think of the quote, 'Everyone is fighting a battle you know nothing

about.' Treat everyone as if your kindness makes a difference... because it does! Both to you and the person receiv-
ing it.

4. **Take Care of Yourself:**...This is my mantra, and I say it
    frequently - In order to grieve fully and avoid secondary
    losses to our health, we must take care of our bodies. Keep
    it simple - water, good sleep & healthy foods!

5. **Hang on to Your Humor:** ...Laughter is so powerful (and
    necessary) for us to heal. It releases chemicals in our bodies
    that help us feel good and reduce tension. Win-Win!

And as a final word on suicidal thoughts, if you do find yourself
sinking repeatedly into a sense of preferring death to living, to choosing
to join your wife over living alone, and to thinking death will solve all
your problems, then please go see a counselor as soon as possible. Give
life a chance by at least talking to someone; you may be surprised to
find that you do in fact have many good reasons for continuing to live.

- ## When Parents Outlive Your Wife

I had to overcome some natural resentment and anger that I felt
when my mom, and both of Theresa's parents, outlived her. I was not
angry with them, but rather at the injustice of her passing while still
relatively young compared to them. I had to watch myself and make
special efforts to keep this anger and resentment from coming out in
my conversations with them.

My mother may have suspected this. Except for one time, she did
not discuss the impacts of Theresa's passing in any detail. I imagine
that for some widowers this might be a major challenge. I encourage
you to talk about it openly with a therapist and get it out of your system
before is causes irreparable harm to your relationship with the parents.

• Does a Lengthy Illness Reduce Deep Grieving?

When a loved one dies after a lengthy illness, those around her might experience something called "anticipatory grief." It suggests that at least some of your grieving might be done in advance of the passing of this person. But the important question at this center of his concept is, "Does anticipatory grief allow you to get some of the grieving 'out of the way' before your loved one actually passes? Does it, in fact, lessen the experience of grief later?"

The fact is that you may grieve her loss incrementally because of the extended illness, but you still have the experience of her death to confront. You cannot grieve the loss fully until the loss occurs.

A long-extended illness that results in inevitable death—one that has long been accepted as the only possible outcome—does allow some to move more quickly through the early and most painful deep grieving cycle. That's not the end of the story, though.

Widows and widowers who have endured a long struggle cannot wait to reengage with life once again. Their reentry into work and social life can be a little shocking to those around them as they expect a long intensive grieving period to follow.

A friend and neighbor of mine lost her husband one month before my wife passed away. Her husband had suffered through two years of declining health resulting from brain cancer. She had long prepared for his death, and she was able to return to work about a week after his death. Neighbors wondered about her quick reentry into the work force, but, after talking to her a couple times I could see that she was in a very different place than I was.

So, yes, you might be able to shorten or bypass some of the deep grieving elements if a lengthy illness results in death, however, you will not escape all of them or grieving in general. You still need to buckle up and prepare for a hard and long ride.

The reality is that over time your grief is likely to become less and less intense, that you will increasingly have more times of happiness and joy, and that you will increasingly find ways to accommodate the ongoing dull throb of grief in the background of your consciousness. It will still be with you every day in some way, but, you can learn to move forward again—if you can learn how to allow yourself to do so.

Chapter 5

Counseling – When and Why

Y ou are going to hurt! Maybe more than you ever have before. If you just bottle this up, if you avoid ever letting it out, if you try to escape the pain, you may blow up and cause long term harm to both you and your loved ones. Please hear me on this one thing: Talk to someone. The sooner the better. Don't be a macho fool. Learn to let it out in controlled and constructive ways that will help you to heal. If you don't talk it out, you very probably will act it out.

Aside from a single visit to a therapist during my teenage years, I had never gone to a counselor before. Even though I worked in a field (social services) where counselors performed a vital role, I still had reservations about my need for such help.

Based on my personal experience and research, men often avoid counseling. As a result, there tend to be few men at the grief groups around the country. Women often outnumber men about 8 to 1 in the coed grief groups. It takes a brave man to go into the usual grief group counseling that is offered in many areas. In the general community, widows outnumber widowers by an average of 4.5 to 1. (Note: This number does not consider the many widowers who remarry within eighteen months of their loss, but who continue to go through their grieving process.) This disparity grows as you look at ratios within counseling groups because women are usually more willing to take advantage of the service, while men often resist this help.

Counseling is critical because there are things that you just don't feel comfortable talking about with your kids, relatives, or friends. If you choose to not talk to anyone about these things, you may delay the grieving process and risk even more severe issues in the future. You are more likely to engage in risky behaviors and/or suicidal thoughts if you do not have an outlet for discussing what you are thinking.

We are men. For the most part, we expect to be able to cope with loss the way we cope with a flood in the basement—by taking action, controlling the situation, and deciding how to solve the problem. We must remember not to apply too much of this ingrained way of thinking upfront to our grieving for a deceased spouse. The old approach might again serve us well later as we move forward, when we are able to put the past behind us at the same time we hold it close to us.

Some people have no choice, but to go back to work, delaying their grieving process until well after the event. In the future, you may regret this, and enter a self-condemnation cycle for not being able to properly grieve for your wife.

I often wondered if I was going crazy during the grieving process. My emotional reactions and anxiety would at times kick into hyper-drive, causing me to doubt my ability to interact with others in a reasonable way. At other times, I just shut down and could not function effectively in terms of performing complex tasks. Sometimes I could do simple repetitive tasks such as organizing all the photos, scanning and organizing them, and sending them out to everyone or posting them on our Caring Bridge page.

Talking to a counselor provided me with an outlet and a way to get things off my chest in a safe place. Through talking with my female counselor, I was even able to laugh at some of my predicaments, which allowed me to put them behind me more quickly and to see just how confused I was.

My therapist provided me with tips on how to deal with some of the issues I was facing, and to provide me with some assurance that what I was going through was normal and that I was not going crazy.

I cannot place enough emphasis on the value of going to a therapist as you proceed along your grieving journey. A common complaint in men's grief groups is that we have trouble with crying. One component of this "trouble" is that we don't know how because we learned through example from other men in our lives to not cry. Another is, as I have mentioned before: Our testosterone level affects our ability to cry. Each man cries differently, so don't get hung up on how much you cry as we are all different.

Many places, such as hospices, provide initial counseling for free and will provide reduced fees for anyone needing this help beyond that portion underwritten by Medicare. Even if you only go once or twice a month, counseling can provide you with invaluable support during this process, and it can offer you a way out of the craziness that at times envelopes your life.

- ## Why Counseling is Important

I heard repeatedly how important it is to take good care of yourself during the grieving period. I found that because I was so disoriented, tired, and sometimes almost delusional, I sometimes could not eat properly, sleep enough, exercise enough, or interact with others well.

The following information is drawn from the widowshope.org website to provide some background and information that will help you to understand why counseling is so important. I have included my own observations following each one.

Death of a spouse is #1 Stressor: Losing a spouse is ranked number one on the stress index scale (Holmes & Raheb Stress Scale), making it one of life's most devastating events. The stress chart assigns a numerical point value to each life stressor. Death of a spouse scores 100 points; a snowball effect of stressors can occur because of the loss.

Scores of 300+ indicate a strong risk of illness. With knowledge and proper care, we can prevent or lessen this statistic: **60 percent** of those who lose a spouse or significant other will **experience a serious illness** in the twelve months following that loss. Those widowed have reported illnesses like cancer and shingles. Widows and the friends and family that love them need to be aware of the snowball effect of such a staggering loss. You are encouraged to take care of yourself!

> **Fred's Response**: True. I had never and never will again experience a more powerful ongoing stress than I experienced after my wife's death. Four months after my wife's passing I went through an emergency hernia operation. Not much later I had an eruption of skin cancer that revisited me in several places. So, I am just another data point in the proof of stress impacts.

Sleep can be severely impacted with the loss of a spouse. Disrupted sleep makes it harder to handle our grief, our lives, and even the day-to-day duties of making beds or paying bills. And, affects our health.

Fred's Response: My sleep was so impacted that there were many nights when I was lucky to get an hour or two of sleep. I avoided asking for or taking any medication until about three months in when I found some decent over the counter medications. (You might ask your counselor or doctor about which might be effective for you with minimal risk of addiction.) Your body and mind are in hyper-drive much of the time and this is aggravated by the lack of sleep, which in turn makes it even harder to sleep. In my case this led to some delusions which presented even greater hazards to my health.

Widowhood increases survivors' risk of dying from almost all causes. In other words, the death of a spouse poses major risks to the health and longevity of the surviving spouse.

Fred's Response: I found a great deal of data online in various articles, research papers, and books backing this up.

On average over 75 percent of the survivor's support base is lost following the loss of a spouse or significant other; including loss of support from family and friends. There are many reasons for losing friends and family such as the loss of couples' friends. We can isolate and be sad and unpleasant to be around. Family members are also grieving and go through unpleasant stages of grief. We take on responsibility, such as taking care of a house and/or children, and life changes in huge ways. We need to build new friendships and support systems.

Fred's Response: You can beat this one. I did. I reached out to others for help, allowed others to reach out to me and let them know that I was grateful for it. One year after her passing I had kept many of my old friends and some of my wife's friends. I actually added new friends by sharing my story openly and honestly, joining groups, and calling/emailing my old friends when I needed to. The Caring Bridge web site helped me to keep everyone in the loop, so they still felt close to me. Eventually, I did become less interactive with my wife's old friends as my other interests and relationships changed.

Be especially aware of possible consequences of bad decisions during this period. If a widower suddenly takes up with another woman too soon after his wife's passing, he risks losing both family and friends quickly and permanently. They can't understand this element of what we go through and may even condemn you for "choosing sex first." This is another vital reason for delaying any major decisions during the first year after your wife's passing.

People who feel consistently lonely have a 14 percent higher risk of premature death than those who don't, according to research. The impact of loneliness on early death is almost as strong as being poor, which increased the chances of dying early by 19 percent, research found. "Loneliness is a risk factor for early death beyond what can be explained by poor health behaviors," says psychologist John Cacioppo, Director of the Center for Cognitive and Social Neuroscience at the University of Chicago.[7]

Also, there really is such a thing as dying of a broken heart. Dr. Suzanne Steinbaum, author of *Dr. Suzanne Steinbaum's Heart Book*, documents the phenomenon and potentially devastating effects of heartsickness in her book. Symptoms of Takosubo's cardiomyopathy (broken heart syndrome) are similar to those of a heart attack and are brought on by a profound sense of stress and loss.

Widows and widowers have a greatly elevated risk of dying in the first six months after a spouse passes away—as high as 30 percent.

Fred's Response: I can see how this could be true. I certainly experienced the shortness of breath, chest pains, an accelerated heartbeat during the early grieving, and I certainly was ready to die and join my wife. There was nothing holding me back except my kids and grandkids. Now that I am in tune with this, I really notice the reports of one spouse dying within hours or days of their partner's death.

Romeo Vitale, PhD, notes in his blog, "Numerous research studies have demonstrated that spousal bereavement is a major source of life stress that often leaves people vulnerable to later problems, including depression, chronic stress, and reduced life expectancy." [8]

> **Fred's Response**: Again, I can see how this can happen, especially if you do not talk to anyone, do not ask for help, and just isolate yourself. The thoughts you have, even when you have this support, are powerful and scary. I found that the sleeplessness issue just magnifies them tenfold.

In summary, there are many potential negative consequences which you may encounter, and counseling can help you to avoid the worst of those possible outcomes.

Humor as an antidote: Not surprisingly, humor is reported to be an effective way to counter and heal the effects of grief. Psychologist Dale Lund (University of Utah) reported that 75 percent of bereaved men and women participating in a survey reported finding humor and laughter in their daily lives at higher levels than they had expected.

In an online AARP article, Ruth Davis Konigsberg, notes:

> Being able to draw upon happy memories of the deceased helps you heal – those who were able to smile when describing their relationship to their husband or wife six months after the loss were happier and healthier 14 months out than those who could only speak of the deceased with sadness, fear, or anger. [9]

Her point is to try to focus on good memories and feelings about your relationship. These positive emotions can protect your psyche and help you find a sense of peace.

Fred's Response: I certainly found this to be true. When I was in a funk, I would sometimes force myself to watch a comedy (*Big Bang Theory* and *Seinfeld* were good go to's) to shake myself out of it. Then, I began to make a more concerted effort to focus on the great and long and rewarding relationship I had with my wife. I created a sheet which I posted above the toilet in the master bathroom, so I would have to look at it every morning when I got up to take a leak. The sheet started with, "Start every day with gratitude for" and then listed my wife, daughters, family, friends, neighbors, workmates, etc. Also, I learned to laugh more at myself and all the delusions and warped sense of things I sometimes had. If you don't learn to laugh a little at yourself, you might go crazy. Laughter is a great counter to all the nagging thoughts that try to constantly drag you back down into grieving.

- ### Where to Go for Counseling

Many area hospices, churches, hospitals, cancer centers, and family services organizations offer grief counseling, often for free for the first few sessions. Their offerings may include individual counseling, small group counseling sessions, and larger groups as well.

I found both small and large groups were heavily weighted towards women, with women outnumbering men from 3 to 1 up to 8 to 1. These numbers are common based on my research. However, as men began to attend our groups, more men felt comfortable with joining the group.

The key to getting value out of these groups is to participate, rather than just sit back and wallow in your grief. As I learned to listen to my fellow travelers, I found that we had some common bonds. Though they were mostly women, they were going through a lot of the same issues. I learned a lot from them in the sense of learning how to share better, how to express my grief, and how to accept compassion. These skills helped me to process my grief more quickly. If you can find a men's grief group, then all the better.

As I wanted to engage with more men during the process, I helped my hospice to form a men's grief group which meets monthly. This group attracted more men into therapy and processing of their grief.

There are great online resources to help you find help, such as:

- National Widowers Association: www.nationalwidowers.org, which lists support groups around the country as well as provides various resources that are helpful.

- Open to Hope: www.opentohope.com offers articles and talks on grief by real people who have experienced the loss of a loved one. They have sections specific to loss of spouse.

- Meetup.com: www.meetup.com provides access to thousands of activities in most areas, including Widow/Widower and Grief groups.

- Center for Loss & Life Transition is dedicated to helping those who are grieving and those who care for them. www.centerforloss.com

- Cancer Support Community: located in many communities, the site is www.cancersupportcommunity.org

- Soaring Spirits International: www.soaringspirits.org provides a variety of online resources

- Hospice Foundation of America: hospicefoundation.org provides information about many hospices around the country and access to online articles about end-of-life and grief

- Online Grief Support: www.onlinegriefsupport.com offers online support including online groups, information about grieving, and even After Death Experiences

- The Good Men's Project: goodmenproject.com offers Mark Liebenow's substantive and helpful writings on grief

- GriefNet.org: www.griefnet.org an online support group that offers specific online groups for loss of spouse or partner

- GriefJourney.com: www.griefjourney.com/wp offers online grief support

- Griefshare.org: www.griefshare.org offers a listing of church-based grief groups in your area

- Grief Support Services.org: www.griefsupportservices.org provides a wide array of online services for fees

- Mygriefangels.org: www.mygriefangels.org is a website listing hundreds of resources, including many specific to certain types of losses

- Modern Loss: www.modernloss.com provides articles written by people like you and me who have gone through the grief process and have something to share: modernloss.com

This list is by no means comprehensive. I encourage you to do your own online research, to speak with your local hospice or church, and to invest in your well-being by asking for help.

- ## Talented Women Therapists Can Help You

In his book, *The Way Men Heal*, based upon his experience in a counseling center for death and dying, therapist Thomas Golden noticed that men differed in how they regarded eye contact and face-to-face therapy as being challenging rather than attentive—rather than being in it together, shoulder to shoulder.

Golden observes that men often feel abandoned after loss, without a sense of safe haven wherein they can start to tell their story—through actions even more than words. He focused on the need to feel that you are in a safe space in order to heal by feeling connected to other people.

Based on his observations, women counselors can be uncomfortable working with widowers, because men grieve differently than the widows they are used to serving. As covered elsewhere in this book, men often experience anger and sexual issues much more prominently than widows. This can be uncomfortable as a counselor may even feel unsafe in a room alone with a grieving widower.

However, I found that there are qualified and dedicated women counselors who have faced the challenges of providing therapy to men before, who have developed the skills to help the man through his grief, and who feel able to treat widowers. Seek them out. Have a candid conversation with the therapist, hospice, or agency you approach about finding the right therapist.

My experience shows that a well-qualified woman counselor can provide you with as good a treatment and support as a male therapist. And in some cases, their support may be even more effective if you give it a chance.

For example, a woman therapist can provide a female perspective on various questions you have about how your wife might feel, about how your daughters might respond, or about how future woman friends might feel about everything from dating to intimacy.

As a widower, I found that you can help the counselor by letting that person know that you appreciate the support and that you are willing to laugh at yourself when your emotions, thoughts, reactions get out of hand either in or out of session.

Based upon many conversations with other widowers, you would be a major exception if you did not feel that you are going crazy at some point, if you did not experience moments of delusion, and if you did not experience some super heightened emotions.

For me, some of this was due to lack of sleep, to stress, and to the huge void that has just appeared in my life. A counselor helped me to see that these symptoms are normal, that I was not going crazy, and provided me with tips on how best to deal with these issues.

I found that just saying it, just sharing it, and opening up to someone about it took a huge burden off my shoulders. I found that a woman counselor was just as capable of helping me through these issues and did so very effectively.

There are many things that I found difficult to talk to my children, friends, fellow employees, and a pastor about, in part because I was not comfortable doing it and in part because I knew they would not know how to react to some of the things I was experiencing.

One option that I found helpful, was I developed two additional "peer" therapists who I could vocalize my thoughts to without fear of embarrassment or ridicule. For me, this included one sister I am very close to who was a therapist herself. Another was my housekeeper, who has a terrific sense of humor and who has an open and frank style of communicating which made me feel safe. They were the ones I could talk to besides my therapist when I just needed to say things to someone and feel supported.

The good news is that, like me, you will get through this in one piece, though you may never feel completely whole again.

Over time, I found that I began to open up to others about the problems I was facing in a way which I never would have considered before.

For example, I found myself able to discuss many of the various emotional and sexual issues with other widowers and divorced men. Though there was some trepidation at first, I gradually became less fearful about sharing with others. In many instances, these men would later express gratitude to me for my openness and for sharing. as they were often experiencing similar issues.

The lessons I learned in these discussions served me well later as I helped to form and then lead a men's grief group at the Pathways' Grief and Loss program.

Chapter 6

Grieving – How Men Differ from Women

You can live, love and have purpose again.

The Hospice of Piedmont notes in an online commentary on Men & Grief,

> When the death of a loved one occurs, the frequently undetected differences between men and women can become quite apparent. As men, we often find it difficult to reach out for help. We tend to avoid admitting we're lost, and we are reluctant to ask for directions. Simply put, we'd rather figure it out ourselves. In many cases, this independence and perseverance serves us well, and we find great satisfaction in triumphing over our challenges. However, emerging research shows that men can benefit from additional support when experiencing the loss of a spouse.

While there are many commonalities between grieving by men and women, there are also some significant differences. Some of these were validated by my experience, others are validated by the experiences of other widowers I either spoke with myself, or who were documented in some of the printed materials I researched for this book.

Thomas R. Golden, LCSW, asserts that roughly 75 percent of men use what he calls the "masculine side of healing," whereas only about 20 percent of women turn to it as their primary mode of healing. More often, women tend to connect with people to facilitate their healing. Men, on the other hand, are often driven "to do things." They have an active response; otherwise, they may find that they are unable to do anything, that is, to have an inactive response.

Anger: Most of my anger was expressed before my wife's death against our local Home Owners Association during a fight over fences. This was an outlet for my frustration at not being able to help my wife. I did not experience major outbursts of anger after her death. That is not to say that I was not mad at God, I was, but it was not a major thing for me. It was not as though I had no regrets about failing to recognize her illness sooner, however, for the most part I was able to acknowledge it and put it behind me. And that is not to say that I did not yell as loud as I could, as I often did during the first few months.

I was mad at the injustice of her passing before me, and at the injustice of death taking a woman I regarded as near sainthood. I did find that many widowers experience severe anger at everything from doctors, to nurses, to clergy, to friends who made well-intentioned but inconsiderate remarks, and at neighbors or friends who failed to support them.

Many of us realize that we have an angry person hiding under the surface. As we mature we learn how to push this "other self" to a hidden place where it is kept under control. However, when you enter the deep grieving process this work can be undone. You may find that you again must learn to tame this "other self" by finding ways to let it out safely, such as going into the forest and yelling as loud as you can.

I did not express anger at friends, neighbors, doctors, health care professionals, and others who I encountered after her passing. I pretty much absolved everyone of responsibility for her death because I saw that was a no-win direction to go. I knew that it would only lead to more stress, more time wasted on unimportant and irrelevant matters, and that it would only be a way to distract myself from the grieving that I so desperately needed to process so I could heal.

Even experienced therapists have problems with widowers' groups. Men and women therapists who have provided support to overcome weight, smoking, alcohol and drug issues often find working with widowers to be particularly challenging. This may be true to a point, but in one men's grief group that I helped to create, I found the men participating to be open, helpful, and willing to listen to each other as well as contribute.

Gratitude as an antidote: I found that constantly reminding myself of how lucky I was to have this wonderful woman in my life for so many years was a great counter to the doubt and anger that tried to suck me into its vortex. Looking back at old photos, talking to friends and family about the good times with my wife, and writing down or recording old memories helped to pull me out of the worst grieving and helped to steer my thoughts away from anger.

Physical Contact and Sex: Based on my own experience and some discussions with widows and widowers, this is an area where there is a dramatic difference between men and women in the grieving process. Men often will rely almost exclusively upon their wife for physical contact ranging from hugs, to hand holding, to rubbing each other's shoulders, and of course for sex. For men (myself included) sex is often the ultimate expression of that physical contact and of love.

A lot of women tend to be more satisfied by hugging, touching, and hand holding as their preferred form of physical contact, especially in the later years. They can get this from many of their girl friends, neighbors, and work mates. So, after the loss of a spouse the void of physical contact is not so pronounced for women as it is for men, who may have few women or guy friends who touch them, much less hug them.

Literally, many men can think about being with another woman within days after their wife's passing as there is such a craving to hold someone in your arms and, yes, to make love to her. I found that the void left by my spouse was so huge and impactful that in my limited capability to think rationally, my mind would go to what it knew best.

During the first months, it was my wife that I fantasized about, but I know I could easily have accepted any woman into my bed, just to have desperately needed physical contact. I know of several widowers who experienced this. If I had done this, I may have deeply regretted it, and it might have set back my healing process. But, I know it could have occurred under certain circumstances—so I don't have a holier than thou attitude about it because I know it can happen.

Over time, hugs from other women, kinds words, and genuine expressions of support can help to reduce this desire. However, at the end of the deep grieving process a whole new set of sex-related issues can emerge that are just as severe and painful, and I do explore these later in the book.

Isolation: While in some ways related to the anger issues, isolation is another problem more common to widowers than to widows. I am aware, though, of several widows who have fallen into this trap as well. For men, it is often directly related to their dependence upon work and wives for social connections. If they are not active in their church, neighborhood, or community, and/or do not have family nearby, these men can be top candidates for falling into severe isolation. This can be evidenced in their staying at home most days, working by themselves, avoiding contact with friends and family, limiting their out of the home activities, and not being responsive to those who do try to reach out to them.

Time, Length and Other Grieving Issues Addressed

- ## Can I Live Again?

In the immediate aftermath of my wife's passing, I had times when I wondered whether life was worth living. The desire to join my wife was strong, and even suicidal thoughts occurred. Death was no longer something to fear, instead I could see how one might welcome it. There were other factors that impacted how strongly I felt, such as:

- Were others dependent upon my ability to remain functional, such as children? This was the biggest factor as I wanted to set a good example for my kids and grandkids, wanted to help them through this, and wanted to be there to help them as their families grew and matured.
- Did I have friends and family to support me through all of this? I was fortunate to have several. If these are not there for you do not be afraid to reach out to those who might be of help.
- Was there a business or community activity that I valued that

was somewhat dependent upon my getting through this? I had left my job to take care of my wife but had a strong interest in being a part of my community through support for area non-profits.

- Did your wife make it clear to you that you had to be strong and continue for the family's sake? My wife and I had talked about this several times long before her death. While our assumption was always that I would be the first to go, we would discuss how we had to be there for the kids after one of us passed. Our running joke was that one of our daughters would throw us into their basement to keep us available for babysitting and cooking duties as needed.

Over time my will to live gained strength. If you are fortunate as I was, family, friends, neighbors and others will offer you much needed comfort and support which makes you feel that life is worth living. However, you can only enjoy this comfort and support if you're willing to accept it. To do so, I needed to let others know that I was open to that support and grateful for it. Like me, you may desperately need to have friends, particularly women, who are brave enough to give you hugs, pats on the back, and kind words. These can become treasured moments that you look forward to and that lift your spirits immensely.

I had woman friends at my granddaughter's preschool, at my former work place, in the neighborhood, at church, and at my wife's craft store. I could always count on at least one or two good hugs to help me get through the day. If I had a day without hugs I was bummed.

As I exited the deep grieving cycle (anywhere from a few months to a year on average) I began to identify those things which can make life fun again. For me this meant new activities (trips, hiking, snowshoeing), new friends, a new woman friend, and new interests such as learning new skills, hobbies, sports, or practices. The spiritual also became increasingly important to me as I looked for answers. I encourage you to open your mind and explore the many different perspectives out there on dying, living, and being a whole and fulfilled person.

I found writings and talks by Deepak Chopra, Eckhart Tollé, and Dr. Brené Brown to be challenging, interesting, and helpful. I adopted the teachings I found useful, and then discarded those I found too far out there or in conflict with my own belief system. Each of those which I adopted made me stronger and better equipped to meet the challenges of grieving.

After a year, I gained the confidence to live life fully again, even though I knew that I would continue to miss my wife, and to grieve for her. You will also find that this kind of research and adoption of new beliefs will bring you into closer contact with other people, including potential woman friends (not necessarily lovers), who can offer you additional support systems going forward. If you are brave, as I was, you may go to group meetings featuring these authors/philosophers and find yourself in a room full of smart attractive women who are only too glad to have an intelligent and inquisitive guy in the group.

- ## Dealing with Crushing Loneliness

Anyone who loses a spouse is going to feel immense loneliness after their death. The longer, better, and/or closer the marriage, the more deeply you may feel that loneliness. For me, it was overwhelming, and my mind just could not believe that it was really true. I would grasp at anything to feel that maybe, just maybe, Theresa was still there with me, even though I knew she was cremated and saw her lifeless body.

For me this took the form of two incidents that gave me a sense of comfort and hope.

1. Two or three days after her passing I was pleading for some sign that she was all right, that she was still with me. Shortly after this, I was making up the bed in the room she had been sleeping in when I felt something on the bottom of my heel. I found a cutout of the word "hello" stuck there.

It had come from her hobby room where she often cut out

words for the many greeting cards that she made by hand. How it had gotten into the bedroom, I have no idea, but to me it was a miraculous and much sought-after sign that she was still with me. I rejoiced and kept that "Hello" on my bathroom counter to remind me that she was still with me in some form or another.

2. A few days later as I sat in my wife's hobby room I was once again pleading for a sign, anything to let me know that she was still with me. At that moment, I noticed a stack of greeting cards that she had been working on shortly before her passing; they were unfinished. I began to look through them, and in the middle, was a Father's Day card she had nearly completed for me (she had her stroke and entered the hospital on Father's Day). The messages on the outside and inside were exactly what I needed to hear at that moment.

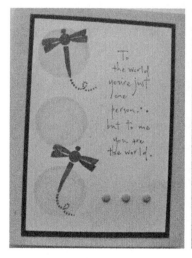 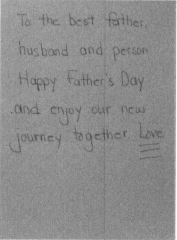

"To the world, you're just one person, but to me you are the world." and "To the best father, husband and person. Happy Father's Day and enjoy our new journey together. Love"

It spoke of how important I was to her, and how much she appreciated me as a husband and person. Perhaps fortuitously it spoke of "our new journey together." Were we still on a journey together after all? Was I mistaken in believing that she was gone? Finally, the card had a blank space where she would normally have signed and spoken of some gift she was giving or promising me. That was left for me to figure out. But, as you might guess, I was very grateful and relieved to find this message from the afterlife if you will.

Many sources document how it is not uncommon for some widows and widowers to report visitations from their spouses in their dreams. These can be very powerful and impactful on the survivor.

As a peer facilitator in a men's grief group, I have heard of "contacts" with deceased spouses, of messages from beyond the grave, of a sense of being directed by a loved one, of meaningful dreams in which a former spouse speaks with them, and of a clear sense of the presence of their spouse.

For the first few months I never had anything resembling this. In fact, for many months I could not see my wife in my mind or in my dreams. This was a huge disappointment to me as I wanted so badly to see her. All I could envision was her in one of the many photographic poses I looked at repeatedly. One of the few dreams I did eventually have with her in it, is documented in an upcoming Caring Bridge entry.

• Sex Drive or Lack of It – What Does It Mean?

Immediately following my wife's death, I was surprised to find that I had a deep craving for physical contact, and more specifically to lie in bed and be with a woman. Other widowers told me that what is most pronounced is the loss of physical contact with your wife and of all future promise of being with a woman again.

Initially I was satisfied with fantasizing about being with my wife intimately again, and due to my slightly delusional state it seemed very real to me. As time passes, you may be glad to have just about any woman lying next to you and satisfying you in that way.

If you have had a long and satisfying marriage, as I did, the thought of going out and recruiting or paying for another woman to lie with you may be unacceptable; so, you don't do it. But, if you were to be offered this opportunity by a friend or acquaintance, there is a very real chance that you would accept the offer due to your desperation.

I know of men who entered relationships as soon as one to three months after their spouse passed, and others who did so around the six-month mark. Generally, but not always, I believe that your chances of having a successful long-term relationship with your new girlfriend are directly related to how long you are willing to wait before entering a new meaningful relationship.

Some will feel guilty, others will not. Either way, I recommend avoiding early relations as they often end poorly for both parties—but not always. In my hyper-emotional state during the first few months after my wife's death I was often making decisions driven more by my emotions and sex drive than by my mind, which often seems to take a hiatus for the duration of the deep grieving cycle.

For those who read this book and don't "get it," I can compare this drive to the male elk who mate themselves into exhaustion during the fall. This often results in their death during the following hard winter. This "rutting" season reminds me of the normal adolescent sex drive that we all experienced in our teen years.

Based on what I have learned and experienced, I would say that choosing a new girlfriend is just one of many major life decisions you want to avoid making during this time. Everything is put at risk by the poor decision- making capabilities you might experience during this period. Your surviving family members and friends may be put off by your actions as well, leaving you with an even smaller support circle.

Of course, there are exceptions to every rule. I know of cases where the surviving spouse turned to her deceased spouse's best friend for support, which turned into love and then marriage that lasted many years. It does happen, but it is the exception, not the rule.

Warning on Pornography: Pornography can be a siren call during this time. I caution you on the poisonous effect it can have on your current and future relationships with all women in your life. I was tempted to view it online, as I know many other widowers are. I quickly realized the corrosive affect this was having on my foundational mores and values.

Why would you support the exploiters of women if you want to love a woman again? Why would you reward revenge postings of women taken advantage of by men who don't know what love is? Don't go down this seductive rabbit hole. This is not you, the loving husband, father, brother your wife loved, cherished, and supported.

Don't turn to those who reinforce negative qualities, who are the antithesis of your wife. I urge you to identify with and reinforce the real you. You know, the one who is the loving husband, father and friend, and hang onto that with all your might. Get together with people who know the real you, and who will reinforce that side of you so you can hang onto that person.

- ## When Does Deep Grieving End?

When I speak of the deep grieving cycle ending, I am not referring to all grieving coming to an end. Grieving in some form is very likely remain with you for years or forever. And, you will have times when deep grieving reappears out of the blue, such as during the year-end holidays. I am referring here to more severe grieving, that time when:
- You seem to still be grieving 24/7; her memory is always near the surface.
- Your physical and mental condition are still raw; crying, sobbing, yelling and/or breakdowns still occur regularly.
- You are still having trouble sleeping most if not all nights unless you take some sleep aids.
- You still have "funk" days, that is days where you are depressed and just do not want to go anywhere.
- You may not be regularly talking out your issues with others, and you may still be relying only on yourself.

The deep grieving cycle ends when it ends. It is different for each of us; it can be as soon as a few months, a year, or last even longer. To put it bluntly, I had no control over it. My conversations with other widowers confirm this. I do know that some men can put it off for a time, but this appears to only delay the inevitable, not to reduce or eliminate it.

I read about a widower who lamented over the fact that the year "anniversary" of his wife's death did nothing more than trigger a new cycle of depression. He entered the Christmas season in a deep state of sadness, unable to function and far from being able to experience any sense of normalcy. That, too, is within the realm of "normal."

My deep grieving cycle ended after five months due to an unusual circumstance (see Caring Bridge #26 on emergency hernia operation). The figure I hear most often from other men is six months, but I've known some who were still suffering deep grief after two years.

I honestly believe it has nothing to do with how much one loved his spouse. I have spoken to several widowers who loved their wives deeply, but still were able to exit the deep grieving within six months to a year.

And I have found the same true with some women I have spoken to, who were able to exit the deep grieving within one to two years. Many widows appear to be comfortable with not entering the dating scene again until several years later, many waiting even longer though they are still attractive and full of life.

From what I have seen and observed, deep grieving beyond two years may indicate other issues that need to be addressed so that person can heal and progress beyond a sense of isolation, dependence, or worthlessness. As women do often seem to take longer than men, don't be put off by this when you meet a widow who is still suffering two to three years into the grieving process.

After talking to many widows, I don't believe that there is any one reason why many grieve longer, or why some never date again. Factors include: how big a support circle they have, fear of dating again, the way women emotionally invest in a marriage, unwillingness to engage in intimacy with anyone else after long relationship with just one man, self-body image and fear of exposing themselves to a man other than their husband, and the fact that widows outnumber widowers 4.5 to 1. Additionally, the numbers of single women over 55 significantly outnumber men in that age bracket.

While based on anecdotal and personal experience, I believe that men more than most women often over analyze things, driving themselves to distraction and not allowing the much-needed emotional processing to take place.

Stop trying to figure out what is the right way or length of time to grieve, and just let it happen. I found that your mind and body are likely to let you know when it is time, if you are listening. This is another reason to meet regularly with a qualified grief counselor who can help you to determine what these messages mean, and when it is the right time to accept that the deep grief cycle has ended.

You do not want to emerge from this cycle and needlessly punish yourself for not thinking about your wife 24/7. Self-condemnation is a nasty and insidious symptom that you must confront and defeat or suffer possible consequences.

Joining grief groups was one way for me to hear other experiences first hand, and to see how I was progressing in relationship to others. I also learned from the stories I heard. Through these stories I picked up tips on how to deal with my own grief experience. I heard of some who were quickly processing their grief, and of others who were still caught in the vortex of grief after more than three years of grieving.

Even after I left the deep grieving cycle, I still experienced the same depth and power of grieving at unexpected moments, such as during holidays and special anniversaries. You are never totally in the clear.

The following blog was my way of addressing the pain I suffered during the deep grieving cycle.

Caring Bridge #17: Surviving the Pain of Loss
by Fred Colby, July 17, 2015

I cannot imagine a pain worse than losing one you have loved and spent at least half of almost every day with for over 45+ years. We are all making progress but have far to go. We each will heal in our own way at our own pace. I am now a lot more empathetic with others who have also lost loved ones. I also better understand what our dedicated military members must go through when they lose close friends in combat. No wonder they often suffer from PTSD, I would too if I had lost

loved ones in such settings.

It makes me even more appreciative of Theresa's dedication to Soldier's Angels for the past 10+ years where she and her many friends prepared and sent cards to individual members of the military who needed a little loving. They also sent packets of beautiful handmade cards to military chaplains who could use them to give out to soldiers either for consoling them or for the soldiers use to send home to their loved ones. Some area friends are continuing this great and kind work in memory of Theresa. They are coming together regularly at Scrap 2 It to make these cards.

Now for those of you who love us and care for us, and who are wondering what the appropriate protocol is around us during this period of grieving, I can tell you that the most important thing is to just let us know you care. And for me at least, I want to talk about Theresa, I want to hear the great stories about her, I want to celebrate those fun and loving moments you had with her.... I don't want to forget her, and I don't care if I cry... It is okay... So, if you can survive my tearing up, go ahead and share. I embrace each moment I get to remember her and honor her. I would rather do that than suffer in silence and keep it all bottled up.

As a long established and well versed "guy" with all the obtuseness expected of such, I can tell you that Theresa taught me over the years to overcome this disease and to be more open to accepting and expressing love... so it does not bother me. I know I have far to go to achieve her level of unselfishness and loving, but, I do aspire to get a little closer to that level every day.

Love you all, thank you. Fred

Comments (A sampling)

Thank you Fred, for your connecting with us today. I can't explain well in words just how much your sharing yourself means to me. There are reminders of Theresa in every part of my craft room. I can only imagine what you have discovered while spending time in hers. My sisters and I were singing hymns to my mother as she exchanged her broken body for one prepared for her in glory. What special moments to remember and even now after these many years, my voice can't sing the

*notes, but my tears can. And I've found that it's really okay. I still love
the hymns. I do pray someone will sing to me some day.* — Sharon K.
*Thanks, Fred - your posts help a lot of us. Hopefully we will be able to
help you. Glad to see you recognize the importance of grieving. Thanks
for sharing about the Soldier's Angels. I can't believe the work she put
into this, and she loved every minute of it. Every time we received one
of her beautiful hand-made cards, I knew that she was sending 50 to
100 to our soldiers also.* — Lin M.

• Activity and Tasks as Self – Therapy

I found one way that men differ from women during the early
grieving process, is that we often retreat into physical activities, tasks,
or projects as therapeutic vehicles for dealing with our grief. For me
this included organizing my wife's craft room, organizing photos, writing my blogs, and working with her friends and my daughters on a
scrap book (see Caring Bridge entry below).

In *The Way Men Heal*, Golden says, "I started noticing that some
people used actions as a means of working with their grief, I began to
see that these actions could be broken down into three basic categories…practical actions, creative actions, and thinking actions."

I completely identified with these types of actions. As you will see
in my blogs I did all three in one form or another. Golden also notes
that men often will dedicate their work or a project in honor of those
they lost. This book and many other things I did after Theresa's passing
fit this description.

Some other projects I have heard about from other men included:
- Writing songs about their experience and setting it to music.
- Reorganizing the wife's knitting room and finishing a couple of
  her knitting projects.
- Making and distributing gifts for family at holiday time.
- Creating memorials to the deceased wife.

Writing a book, blogs, or articles is not an uncommon way to process the grief. For me, writing this book was very therapeutic, but it
was also painful. Each time I wrote, reviewed or edited a portion of it,
old memories and pain would come flooding back to me. It forced me

to confront all kinds of questions and fears—as well as tears. Over time I came to appreciate this as part of the healing process.

A fellow widower, Robert Devereaux, whom I met through counseling groups at Pathways, recounted how he dealt with the grief in his own way:

> I had two major therapeutic outlets for coming to terms with my grief, beyond the absolutely central and critical task of sitting quietly with my grief, inviting it to break bread with me, and welcoming it, warmly but with regretful reluctance, as a new and valued friend. Loss is an integral part of life, and grief has much of value to give one, even after a terrible loss
>
> My first outlet was attending grief support groups at our local hospice organization, the same agency that had seen my beloved through her final weeks of life, so helpful in so many ways. They offered a group for the newly bereaved and, some months later, one called Writing through Loss. It was a privilege and a gift to sit with people who had suffered a similar loss. In such groups, there's no need to hide or mute one's feelings out of a sense of social propriety. Those hours huddled together—hours of quiet empathy and witnessing—were sacred in the deepest sense of that word.
>
> My second outlet came through acting onstage. Throughout my life, theatre has always granted me its cherished gifts. But acting the side-of-the-stage narrator in a readers' theatre production eight weeks after Victoria's death blessed me in special ways. Live theatre, by its very nature, intimately celebrates life in the midst of a temporary-yet-intense community of actors that forms during the weeks of preparation and performance. But its gifts greatly intensify during a rough emotional patch. And so, it was for me.

The following Caring Bridge entry demonstrates some of my own therapeutic activities and why they were so important to my healing.

Caring Bridge #16: Still Doing Projects for Theresa
by Fred Colby, July 26, 2015

One way I find sanity through all of this is to find new projects that are centered on Theresa. In the past, I had often grumbled, stalled, and complained about some of the projects Theresa dreamed up for me (see backyard cleanup, garage, basement, craft room, etc.). The reality is that I loved doing them for her. She always appreciated the outcome (you all can picture her look of outright joy).

So, in her absence I continue to find new projects. I've cleaned up her craft room, reorganized some of it to help Charlene and Jennifer to find things, and am in the process of creating a Tribute Wall for her in the craft room. I have posted a few more photos I found, one of her as a baby, one of our couple shots, and one from her prom night.

I went to church for first time in months today and could not make it through the hymns. They were the same hymns I was singing to her as she passed. Overall, I am making some progress, but moments of remembering come out of nowhere and loneliness hits hard, such as when I bought groceries for just a $31 total... hard to buy for one now.

Comments (A sampling)

It takes so much longer than you think it will, and it hits in waves in the strangest places and situations. But the only way out is through, as you encounter the endless realizations of how different your daily life is going to be from now on, and how interwoven you two were from the decades of adjustments and compromises you made to each other to live together so successfully. Much love to you. — Ann C.

Beautiful post Fred. Theresa is surely smiling knowing you are hard at work on all those projects. May you continue to find comfort in Theresa projects and remember you are surrounded by love and support. — Mary R.

Caring Bridge #17: Theresa's Tribute Wall
by Fred Colby, August 6, 2015

This is one of my "sanity" projects to keep her memory alive for me and the kids while giving me something constructive to do. I also found two boxes of slides from our 1972 post-college graduation trip to Europe and a later Hawaii trip. Had to go out and find something to convert slides to digital so I can share them with the daughters and others. That will keep me occupied for quite a while. Hope to find a few jewels in those boxes.

I was busy Monday through Wednesday, finally got to slow down today... I know that means more time grieving as you are not distracted with all the busy stuff, but, I know that I must go through it, can't just avoid it... It catches up to you no matter what... again, and again.

Next week Jen, Charlene, the grandkids and I are going together to work on a scrapbook of all the beautiful cards sent to Theresa and us during this ordeal. Hoping it gives the kiddos some closure too.

Tina B. graciously had us all over to look at her stamping room. I wanted the girls to get some ideas of how we might organize mama's craft room, so they could find things better, and have more workspace.

This was one of the projects Theresa and I were hoping to tackle after her treatment, so glad to at least get some of it in place for the girls and grandkids.

Tina G. has taken over Theresa's role with Soldiers Angels to co-ordinate the making and distribution of cards to many soldiers serving overseas. Theresa would get the nicest notes back from many of them who were so grateful to get a nice card and best wishes from someone they did not even know. Several exchanged letters and cards with her over the years.

- ## How You Remember Your Wife

As I processed my grief, I found myself struggling to remember my wife in meaningful ways. My memory was fuzzy, I could not see her in my thoughts or dreams, and I was having delusional thoughts which stopped me from thinking clearly.

Theresa's photos, videos, letters, and other writings became my primary links to her and her memory. I realized I honored her every time I remembered her. I would desperately seek these memories.

Like me, you may continue to look for ways to remember and memorialize your wife and her life. I was still having trouble seeing her in my mind or dreams after 10 months of grieving. Waking from a dream that included her in any way is still a reason for celebration.

Idealization of Your Spouse: Based on research and discussions, idealization of the spouse is very common during the grieving process. My family, friends, neighbors and I all tended to remember only the best about Theresa. Whatever so called deficiencies your wife may have (warts, weight, bad behaviors, cleaning, spending habits, etc.), they all fade into the background. Suddenly she is a saint without fault or blemish. Of course, in many ways she was—she put up with me for a ridiculous number of years!

Only time will allow you to see her once again as she was, beautiful blemishes and all. You just cannot maintain the beatified state of belief forever. If you don't learn to see her warts and all, you may have trouble emerging from your grief into a healthier place. I made progress when I became willing to laugh as I remembered those faults and recognized them as just being a part of who she really was to me. This allowed me to continue loving her in a healthier way.

For example, I loved my wife dearly, but, she wanted to travel less and less as we matured—something I loved to do. She was perfectly happy staying in Fort Collins with her family and friends. She no longer enjoyed going out for a nice dinner, the movies, plays, or band performances. Our lives had in many ways settled into a routine that was at best boring and lacking in new challenges or experiences. But I loved her so much that I accepted it and did not push her on it. I cannot tell you how many other widowers have told me of similar experiences.

After her passing I joined several groups and their activities, and began planning more trips, and pushed myself out of our house as often as possible. You will find this necessary to escape the oppressive loneliness that you encounter at home, to help fill the void left by her passing, as well to engage with life again. At first it may seem somehow unfaithful, but I found it helpful to my healing process.

Remembrance Techniques: There may be other ways for you to remember or communicate with your spouse in a way helpful to your healing. Alexandra Kennedy, MA, MFT, in her book, *The Infinite Thread: Healing Relationships Beyond Loss*, speaks about how we can reconnect with our loved ones in creative ways that can help us to heal unresolved issues and move forward after losing a loved one. She shows how to do this by:

- Using imagination to recreate a relationship with a lost loved one to heal unresolved issues and regrets
- Creating a simple sanctuary to give form and beauty to the healing process

- Tapping the power of our dreams to rebuild our own lives
- Learning about ancient, tried and true methods for easing the burdens of grieving
- Finding joy in our daily lives even as we honor our loss.

Exploring new ways to communicate in your imagination or dreams can be a positive way to deal with doubts, regrets, or possibly even fears. Talking to my wife aloud and knowing what her answer would be was one effective way for me to keep her alive and as a part of my life. I found that this helped me to think things through as if she was still there consulting with me on important decisions.

The following Caring Bridge entries address my struggle to go back in time and remember her faithfully.

Caring Bridge #18: Theresa and Me
by Fred Colby, August 10, 2015

I found a couple more fun photos. The first is a photo of me that I sent to Theresa just to show I did have a sense of humor at age 21. My friend Marty and I had set out on an epic last trip as best buds before Theresa and I really got serious. We were visiting Colorado and with this photo I was prompted to play off the "Butch Cassidy and the Sundance Kid" movie of the time. The note invites Theresa to join Marty, his girlfriend Pam, and me in Bolivia as we weren't doing too many jobs at the time.

During that trip, we enjoyed backroad chases involving locals, run downs of peeping toms, car breakdowns in the middle of the desert, sleeping bags on ant hills, and visits with all kinds of interesting people. The second photo is of Theresa and Ken Norton during his heyday as one of very few fighters who beat Cassius Clay, known shortly thereafter as Muhammad Ali. A friend of Theresa's persuaded her to go down and get autographs and of course Theresa got him to pose for a photo too. Whoever resisted her requests? Not many!

Caring Bridge #19: Theresa's Friends
by Fred Colby, August 16, 2015

Pictured here are a few of Theresa's close Fort Collins friends. Everywhere we went Theresa formed new and long-lasting friendships, many of which lasted a lifetime. Her nineteen closest local friends were so generous with their love and support during Theresa's ordeal and passing that she and the rest of her family felt encircled by love throughout and after.

Last week many of her friends joined us at Scrap 2 It to make a Theresa Scrapbook which includes many of the loving cards sent to her during her treatment. My two daughters and four grandkids joined us and by day's end we had nearly 20 pages put together.

More are being worked on at home and I will go to the store on Wednesday to gather those up and put a scrapbook together. I finished four pages by myself! Theresa would be surprised and pleased.

This circle of friends that stretches from San Diego to Portland to Nebraska and to Colorado is an unbelievably loving group which I am in awe of and forever grateful to for befriending my Theresa.

Comments (A sampling)

She was so friendly and fun to be around! I know how much her friends in Fort Collins, and all her scrapbooking/card making friends meant to her. She told me how great it was to get out when (during her chemo treatment) her friends got together for lunch. Thank you all. — Lin M.

Caring Bridge #20: Becoming a Master Card Maker
by Fred Colby, August 19, 2015

Nearly 20 years ago, Theresa faced a new life after dropping off our youngest daughter, Charlene, at Occidental College to start her own new future. Theresa cried most of the way home from Los Angeles to San Diego, with my having to pull off the freeway so we could talk things through. Much like I feel now with the void left in my life, she could not imagine going forward without her daughters in her everyday life.

After the birth of Jennifer and then Charlene, nothing gave her greater pleasure than being a mom, and in being a part of her children's lives. You can always tell the parents who really enjoy their roles, and Theresa did that.

After Charlene started college Theresa started to work more and more at LPL in a clerical job she secured with the help of our good neighbor, Jan H. She made many fast and long-time friends at LPL, some of whom I hope to see while in San Diego next week. Michelle and Dave traveled to Colorado with us on a great trip which saw Dave and me catching over 200 trout in a week's time (yes, catch and release except for an unlucky few who got to become dinner).

Many others were regulars at our house for gatherings, including our famous annual New Year's Eve tamale party.

However, the one thing she turned to more than ever was card making. She started to attend more classes, to make more friends in the field, and to make more professional and creative cards. For nearly 20 years card making became her outlet for expressing her joy, creativity and love for her family, friends, and community.

I now have over 3,000 cards that she made sitting in her craft room. My thought is to begin sharing these out, as to leave them sitting in drawers never seeing the light of day seems a travesty. I want her to be able to continue sharing that love and creativity with those she cared about.

Comments (A sampling)

She was an amazing mom and I was so lucky to have her care SO much for Jennifer and me. We were extremely blessed to have a mom who wanted to spend so much time with us. I am grateful for the standard she has set, and I know my children will benefit from that. I know I'll be just like her on the first day of college, bawling my eyes out while bidding farewell to my angels. — Charlene O.

Fred, I can't tell you how much your posts mean to me. It is so wonderful to share in a part of Theresa's life that I didn't know about. She will always be close to my heart and now in new ways. — Joy S.

- **Revisiting Old Memories, Places & People**

As I progressed in my grieving process I often felt the siren call of wanting to revisit not only the old memories of our early courting and marriage, but also the things, places and people who were important to us during those early days.

Her Clothes and Possessions: One quandary I faced was how to deal with her clothes hanging in the closet and in the dressers, as well as her shoes, jewelry, purses, and toiletries. The disposing or giving away of each of these can present its own challenge. At first it literally felt as if I was giving away a piece of her and a piece of me. It hurts! I recommend you don't start this until you feel ready to do so. I know widowers who waited two to three years before tackling this. Take your time, yet be conscious that the longer you hang on to them, the longer it will take you to emerge from the grief into a more interactive healthier place.

My approach was to begin with those things to which I was least attached, so first the toiletries, then the items in the drawers that I knew were not important to her. This was followed by shoes and purses, and then in stages her clothing starting with the ones she wore the least (many new never worn items first) and then lastly jewelry and those clothes I remembered her in best.

This took over a year, starting about three months after her passing. In every case I invited the daughters over to go through and find those items they wanted to save, to give to their kids, or to make pillows out of. The rest I donated to causes such as domestic violence shelters that I knew my wife would have appreciated helping.

One humorous outcome of this process was that we found two stashes of cash (totaling over $500) that Theresa had hidden for her two secret passions: buying surprise gifts for the grandkids and making an occasional trip to the area casinos. My daughters and I got quite a kick out of these finds.

People and Places: For me, this included visiting our wedding place, old haunts in San Diego, and of course family and friends. I prepared myself emotionally (this was two months after her passing) for what I expected would be a major grieving event. The anticipation of the trip ended up being rougher than the trip itself.

The following Caring Bridge entries outline my experience.

Caring Bridge #21: Wedding Photos and Visit
by Fred Colby, August 23, 2015

Well, I am on my way to San Diego and during my visit plan to walk over to the site of our wedding on Coronado. Looking back at some of the photos I posted, I can't help but think it was the best day of my life and the best decision I ever made. I am so grateful to have had this amazing woman in my life and know I will miss her every day until I join her. As usual Theresa's smile is tight lipped in these photos before she got braces during our 2nd year of marriage. After the wedding, that was our second-best decision as she smiled from ear to ear after that. I never did notice her teeth being at all crooked, but she was very self-conscious about it.

I know it will be painful to go to the wedding location (which may or may not be there anymore) but feel driven to do these little things to stay just a little closer to her.

Comments (A sampling)

It was a beautiful site, beautiful day and the beginning of a beautiful life. A very fun event for all of us. You two look so... seventyish! Ha! And so happy. I never knew Theresa had crooked teeth either – of course, I did also. Maybe that is why we never talked about it. (I got my braces when I was in my 50's.) Enjoy your visit to San Diego and good memories. Linnie — Lin M.

Caring Bridge #22: Visiting Home & Wedding Site
by Fred Colby, September 1, 2015

The trip was not what I expected! This photo is of the Coronado Bridge near my hotel at night. I then visited where I thought the Coronado Women's Club was when we were married. What I found was a parking lot where the Women's Club was at one time located. It was torn down years ago, and the City Hall, Rec Center, and theater built in its place... along with a marina. The final photo is of my writing her name on the Coronado shore to be washed away over time.

The trip was very different from what I thought it might be. My several reunions with close friends and family were more celebrations, therapy, and sharing rather than pain and sorrow. And the visit to our wedding spot was a total non-event. No emotions at the absence of our marriage site, nothing except fulfilling a goal of mine to find out what had happened to it.

Meeting with Michelle & Dave, Maria & Evonne, Bob & Cathy, Karen & Tim, and with Joann and my family were much more impactful and meaningful than anything else could have been. With some, I could share their loss experiences which provided additional support and guidance for me going forward.

I was fortunate to spend some time with Theresa's brother, Robert, and her parents. Her mom who has been experiencing an onset of dementia herself recognized me right away and ran up to hug me, and it was rewarding for me to be there to help them out with some things. Bob G. was wonderful in helping Theresa's brother with some loan documents and papers.

Finally, the biggest takeaway for me from this trip was that I realize a little more every week that Theresa just is not in the things or places that were at one time important to us.

As much as I try to find her there, she just isn't. The only things that are meaningful in any way are the photos and her cards as they stir up wonderful memories... the photos for the memory of things done together and the cards for the thoughts she expressed... which is as close as I can get to her soul or substance.

Reality settles in like a dripping faucet filling a bucket over time, eventually you get there and must let something out to make room for the new realities coming in. Not sure how that is all going to work out, just know I must keep on going to find out.

Comments (A sampling)

Fred, it meant so much for Dave and me to be able to spend time with you. Reminiscing about Theresa (Mama Bear) and all the good times we shared with both of you was very special. The impact she made on so many lives says so much on the kind of person she was. We are all here for you and the girls and love you all very much! — Michelle P.

Welcome home my friend and your comments were certainly heartfelt. Somehow time helps in finding "new normals"... don't rush it but trust me in that it will happen! Life will never ever be the same as you once knew it but somehow, we survive. — Carol F.

- **Surviving Anniversaries and Birthdays**

I experienced my first passage through our Wedding Anniversary only ten weeks after her passing. I was dreading it for over a month and feared a complete regression to my very first week of grieving. To counter this I immersed myself in projects which honored her and helped me to keep the best parts of our marriage in the forefront.

As with the earlier examples of post death "messages" from my wife, I was blessed to find another example of being led to celebrate our marriage in a memorable way that helped me to survive the day. While I grieved deeply for her that day, I was able to come out of it with a sense of gratitude for our marriage which helped me to come out of the grieving in a positive place.

The following Caring Bridge Entry outlines my experience that may give hope to others that there are messages all around us, just waiting to be uncovered.

Caring Bridge #23: 45th Anniversary & Flamingos
by Fred Colby, September 13, 2015

45 years ago, today I was fortunate enough to marry Theresa Frances Bolata after a 2-year courtship. Not too many years later I took one of my favorite photos ever while visiting the Wild Animal Park in northern San Diego. After making a couple prints I lost that slide and could never find it again, then the prints were lost as well.

Today as I was remembering Theresa and all the great times we had together, I went through an old box of slides I found in the basement. Out of literally hundreds (if not thousands) of slides, I found a few which were worth converting to digital images.

In the very last box and in the very last slide I found my missing Flamingo slide. Well, I am always looking for messages in things such as this, and the obvious one is that I was meant to find this at this time as a symbol of our everlasting love as vowed on this day 45 years ago.

Flamingos are one of a few animals that usually mate for life, and this beautiful photo wonderfully symbolizes the beauty and synchronization of lives well lived. What a great way to close off this anniversary day! I have gone from depression to celebration with yet one more inspiring message. I know there will be more tough days, but, this and other support keep lifting me up when needed most. Thank you!!

Comments (A sampling)

A very lovely and inspirational discovery! Surely angels lighting your pathway forward.... Reminding us that nothing of value, including love, can ever be lost! Blessings to both of you. — Kate C.

How wonderful, Fred – to find these on your anniversary. Definitely, a higher power at work here! So glad it lifted your spirits on a difficult day. — Lin M.

Fred: I believe that your beautiful wife "visited" with you today with this amazingly significant find! So thankful that you shared it with us! Just wonderful! Love You, — Rita H.

- ### Expressing Your Grief in New Ways

Besides the activities/tasks/projects that I engaged in to help me process my grief, I found myself looking for other outlets to express that grief. For me it took the form of writing a Dr. Seuss-like poem to communicate my grief in a way which I could share with others.

I have met widowers who have expressed their grief through writings, acting in plays related to grieving, painting, sewing, knitting, and songs. The hospice we worked with, Pathways Hospice, offered several vehicles for expressing mine and my family's grief through art and song. This included making a wreath for the holidays with my wife's pictures and craft items on it, singing a song which incorporated some things specific to her, a butterfly release, and the creation of slide shows.

We each must find our own unique way to express our grief, a way that means something special to us and/or our family. I encourage you to allow yourself to explore innovative ways of expressing yourself that maybe you would never have thought of before. This may build on a talent you have such as writing, singing, writing music, painting, or even carpentry work.

There are no limits on what you can do to create something meaningful and long lasting as a tribute to your wife and your life together. It might be something that your wife did, such as my wife's card making.

The following Caring Bridge entry was my most expressive way of honoring her and the process I was going through.

Caring Bridge #24: I Do Not Like This At All
by Fred Colby, September 23, 2015

Being a former San Diegan and fan of Dr. Seuss, this poem expresses for me what many go through...not exactly prime poetry, but accurate.

I DO NOT LIKE THIS AT ALL
(a Seussian take on the loss of your spouse by Fred Colby)

I do not like this at all
She left me with no place to fall
And now I cannot even call
So now what do I do

I do not like this at all
There is a hole in my house
There is a hole in my heart
There is a hole in my life
And there is no one who can fill it at all

I do not like this at all
I am eating all alone and what I eat does not sound so neat
I have nowhere to go and am tired of watching t.v.
And there is little hope it will get better soon

I do not like this at all
At night, I wake up at all hours
Each day, I need a list to remember what to do and where to go
And then I wait till it is time to sleep again

I do not like this at all
I cannot remember her face
But I remember her all too well, and I remember too well...
That she is not here, and never will be here again.
No, no . . . I do not like this at all.

Comments (A sampling)

Grief is a tricky thing; as soon as you think you're managing it a little,
it shapeshifts into a new form, kicks you in the gut and demands not to
be rushed. It's a lonely, individual journey, reminding you of the great
strengths of your relationship. Sending you lots of love. — Ann C.

Love you dad! You know your girls are always ready to welcome you
into our homes for hugs and grandchild distraction. But we also re-
spect your need to just be alone sometimes. It's ok if your needs change
day to day, hour by hour, just let us know. Xoxo — Charlene O.

Fred: This is one of the saddest, most honest poems I have ever read! I
can't even begin to imagine what it must be like, even though; I can
only imagine what it must be like! (Does that make sense?) Because,
things like death don't make sense, no matter how much we know that
life is a circle. Love — Rita H.

- ## Revisiting the Past

One theme that ran through my entire grieving process, especially during the first few months, was a constant need to go back and revisit the past. This does not need to be a depression routine, which is when you focus entirely on the loss rather than on the great memories. The best way to deal with the temptation of depression for me was to remember the great times while I was looking at the photos and celebrating all of them! I found it helpful to counter the vortex of grief with gratitude for all the good we experienced with each other.

Yes, it will be painful! Yes, you will cry! But that is okay. It is part of the grieving process, and you honor your wife when you remember her this way. I learned to focus on giving thanks for all the great years we had, rather than going deep into depression over her loss.

The following Caring Bridge Entries record some of this process.

Caring Bridge #27: Earliest Photo of Us
by Fred Colby, October 6, 2015

I came across this first existing photo of Theresa and me during our early dating stages. We were visiting friends who had recently had a baby.

We must have been all of 21 and 20 years old ourselves. It looks like two teenagers with a baby at best.

Neither of us wanted children early on in our relationship; both wanted to wait until we were old enough, financially set enough, and mature enough to handle it all. We enjoyed the first carefree years to-gether, with Jennifer coming into our lives about five years after get-ting married.

We were very blessed to have been able to raise our daughters, Jennifer and Charlene, in San Diego where we had family and friends to help us through the process. Next to our decision to marry, our next best decision was to buy a home in Scripps Ranch, a northern suburb of San Diego.

My sister, Ann, helped us to find and purchase a home on Avenida Magnifica, where we lived for 20 years. We had a 12% interest rate on a loan issued during the peak of inflation in 1985. We paid $165,000 for a 2400 sq. ft. home, the same amount we owed on it when we sold it 20 years later!!

Scripps Ranch turned out to be a wonderful area for all of us, with the children blossoming in the area schools, Theresa finding new ways to grow in independence & confidence by volunteering in the schools and local organizations, and a great place for me to learn some leader-ship skills as I jumped into various political/community activities which resulted in my being elected to the San Diego Community College Board. Most importantly, we formed lasting friendships with many neighbors including ones that my daughters continue to treasure and renew on a regular basis.

I've heard from many of Jennifer and Charlene's friends who loved coming over to our house. Mama Theresa would make them feel at home and loved, feeding them with homemade treats. They felt com-fortable talking in front of her as she would go about her business as if she did not hear them. She learned a lot by driving car pool as the girls would chatter unreservedly while going from place to place. Theresa touched many of their lives through her unselfishness and kindnesses.

Caring Bridge #28: Why We Loved Oregon
by Fred Colby, October 13, 2015

Theresa and I moved to Oregon in 2005 after having visited there the previous 2 years. We loved its beauty, the waterfalls, the coast, the flower gardens, the berry farms, and everything was just green green green. Portland was a hoot, one of Theresa's oldest friends lived there, cost of living was much lower than San Diego, and the unbelievably beautiful coast was within an hour's drive.

We moved into a new home with me continuing with my consulting practice from home, and Theresa going to work at an area LPL office where she made a whole new set of friends. We bonded with our neighbors, particularly Jim & Yihua who went on extensive berry hunting trips with us. There were lots of fun and different restaurants to go to. Our favorites included a great Dim-sum place and a Hawaiian BBQ in an older district. Shortly after we moved there, our daughter Charlene got married and moved to Fort Collins. Jennifer visited her the next year and decided to move there also. We followed in 2008.

- **Losing Your Memories and Images**

One major frustration that I incurred big time, was a failure to be able to see my wife in either my thoughts or dreams. After she passed, I could not see in my mind the real Theresa, except for my death bed memories. Photo images, those I looked at most frequently, were the only way I could visualize her.

No matter how hard I tried to remember her, I could at best re-

118

member a feeling of her presence or a sense of her. I could not visualize us walking hand in hand down the beach, her sitting next to me on the sofa, or her face when I spoke to her. It was frustrating as hell!

To top it off, you may well find that you never see her in your dreams no matter how much you want to see her. Over the first six months I had only one brief glimpse of her in one very meaningful dream. After that I had the sense of her being in the dream with me but did not actually see her. Again, it was very frustrating.

The following Caring Bridge entry explains my experience in fuller detail.

Caring Bridge #29: On Dreams, "We," & Grieving
by Fred Colby, October 22, 2015

I have told many that since her passing I have not been able to see Theresa in my mind or my dreams. This was totally disconcerting at first, but, I have been told that this is a normal reaction by the brain. Part of this I think is me not being able to decide which image of my Theresa over our many years together, best represents where she is now, and realizing that maybe none of them do, as she (and we) are really a composite of everything that has gone on before and what may be coming in the future.

In other words, there is no real separation between them in time, they are all NOW, an ongoing circle of life and we just can't see it all at once... but it is continuing.

So, to top this thought off, I finally had a brief sighting of Theresa in a dream. As I woke up one morning a week ago, I had the very clear image of Theresa waiting for me, sitting in one of those old fold-up aluminum and plastic strap picnic chairs as I was walking towards her.

I had the distinct impression that I had dropped her off, gone and parked the car, and was walking to join her before we walked together into an event of some kind, like a music festival. She was wearing a long brown/blond wig (one of several she had, and the one I liked the least but which she seemed to enjoy because of its different look). She looked much like she did during her last year.

Upon waking up I realized that the dream had a much deeper meaning for me... That this image was her way of telling me that she would patiently wait for me, and that when my time comes she will be there to walk with me together on our "new journey" which she re-ferred to in her last Father's Day card that she left for me.

In talking with my counselor/therapist (yes, I have one of those and am grateful to have this support right now) she took it one step farther, saying she thought this was Theresa's way of saying that it's okay for me to get on with my life and regardless of how long it will be, she will be there for me when it is time to move on. I like that thought, a good one to hold on to.

Finally, the other piece to all this is my realization from going through all this process is that there is no "her" and "I" anymore. Over 47 years together so much of her became a part of me, and I am sure much of me became a part of her. So, moving forward, there is only "We." She helped to make me who I am today, and the best way I can honor her is to love and appreciate that part of her that now sur-vives in me, and to remember to draw upon those special traits, values, and ways of thinking as I interact with others and develop new friend-ships moving forward.

I love her as dearly as I did 10, 20, 30, and 40 years ago; and, I know the grieving will be with me in one form or another forever going forward... But, I also know I must reengage with "LIFE" and find new ways to get out and be active again, be it through work, volunteering, joining groups, taking classes, being with my grandkids, or taking trips.

It won't all happen overnight, but, I am committed to reengaging more and more over time as I know Theresa would want me to (yes, we talked about all of this too before she passed and previously when I thought I was a goner 5-years before).

Thank you all for your love and support through all of this, and know that I am praying that every one of you who are in a relationship of any kind will take one thing away from my various musing over the past few months... that is to love and appreciate your partner every day, to express that love verbally and physically (yeah, hug them, touch them, pat them on the butt, and kiss them) every day, and to thank God for the blessings you have and to share your blessings and empathy with as many people as you can.

Going forward I don't know if and when I will write more of these, it will just depend on what little Eureka's I have... but I do know that writing these have been amazingly therapeutic for me and am grateful others have found them to be of value too. We all are grieving for this loss and will for a long time to come, and I thank you for joining me on this journey, because I needed others to support me through it all.

Love you all, Fred

Comments (a sampling)

Thanks Fred once again, for bringing us into this most intimate place with you. Your journey and your words bless me greatly. – Sharon K.

I'm so glad you got to see her in a dream, I've had numerous ones with her and she is always taking care of me in them. The latest one she was quite disappointed in how empty your refrigerator was and was very worried because me and the kiddos were eating all your food. Sounds like mom! Love you Dad — Charlene O.

Fred your posts are so therapeutic for all of us, and I hope that you continue to share with us as you travel this road. Theresa will always continue to be a part of me... the very best part. — Joy S.

As previously mentioned, Alexandra Kennedy in her recent book, *The Infinite Thread: Healing Relationships Beyond Loss*, offers tips and guidance on how to open yourself up to dreams, to remember them and to understand them. These dreams can be very comforting, as mine was to me.

These dreams can help to resolve questions you may have about your relationship with your wife, and help to confront doubts, fears, and regrets that you may be carrying consciously or unconsciously. Some therapists, such as Kennedy, can help guide you on your quest to experience, recall and understand your dreams.

- ## Holidays – Landmines on Path to Recovery

Everyone will start to tell you within a week of your wife's passing that you must steel yourself against the trauma of upcoming special days, including, but not limited to: Wedding Anniversary, Birthday, Thanksgiving, Christmas (or other religious holidays), New Year's Eve, and any other days of import to you and your wife.

My experience was unique to me, as I am sure yours will be for you. Much of your reaction will depend upon how important each of those days was for you and your wife. For example, Theresa and I had gotten to the point that our birthdays were not a big deal to us, so I did not have a major reaction on that day. Same was true for Valentine's Day for me.

However, Thanksgiving and Christmas were major markers for me and did cause a regression to deep grieving. To counter the anticipated Thanksgiving impact, I took our kids and grandkids for an overnight stay at a resort that had a Thanksgiving special buffet. It changed things up enough that the impact was reduced.

Unfortunately, Christmas was as advertised, with my regressing to the worst stages of my grieving as if I were once again in month one of the process. This included full blown meltdowns, sobbing, crying, yelling, and the whole bit. Total funk days occurred often and I could barely function at times.

This Caring Bridge Entry recounts my experience in more detail.

Caring Bridge #30: Surviving the Holidays

By Fred Colby, December 5, 2015

This photo was taken last year (2014) on Christmas morning with Cecilia and newest grandchild, Keira at Charlene's house. Theresa looked great and was still smiling. However, she was unable to attend the afternoon gift exchange at Jennifer's house. She was tiring easily, and not looking forward to surgery five days later just before New Year's Day. This began the six-month ordeal that culminated in her passing at the end of June.

As I now put up the tree, hang the wreath, set out the Christmas displays, and prepare to decorate the tree with my grandchildren I cannot help but remember back to all the great Christmas days of the past. Our family always had a ball during Christmas with lots of meals, presents, and love. I cannot relate to families that struggle and fight over Christmas... don't even know what that would look like. Even the new boyfriends and girlfriends and other guests who were invited to join us fit into the group and were welcomed with open arms.

Theresa loved her family and loved my family without reservation, enjoying the unique qualities of each family member. I know that they all will miss that this year, as I will.

Thanksgiving was tough, but I survived... having my meltdown the day before instead of on the day of Thanksgiving. Having the family together in a different place (Cheyenne Mountain Resort) worked well. We had a great time and did not have constant reminders of Theresa around all day.

For Christmas and New Year's (Theresa's favorite holidays) I will not be so lucky... as the reminders started today with the decorating. I felt it necessary to do this to let the grandkids know that Popa has not forgotten Gaga, and that Christmas goes on no matter what the circumstances.

One thing I have learned during this process is that it is best to confront your demons, your grief, rather than try to avoid it. That does not mean wallowing in constant self-pity where you are reexperiencing the pain for the pain's sake, but, rather allowing your grief to progress and come out as it needs to process your feelings and love for your lost one. Once done, it is much easier to move on and celebrate the good moments from the past and enjoy the ones in the present.

My mantra remains: Stop thinking about yesterday, focus on today, and look forward to tomorrow. I know Theresa would be there with me every step of the way with this approach. God, I miss her... but, am gradually moving on as I know she would have wanted me to.

I continue to be so grateful for all the love and support that has come my family's way since her departure and know that has helped me to heal more quickly. Thank you all.

Caring Bridge #31: Great Memories from 2003
By Fred Colby, December 13, 2015

As we muck our way through these year-end holidays (imagine walking through 2 feet of molasses) and as we try to counter all the reemerging negativity that comes with grief, I escaped again to the photo albums to try and counter it with the positive memories of Theresa and her special spirit.

These photos exemplify her great spirit of love and joy in all things. The first is of our whole family at a 2003 fundraising event (Charlene's date is Chad pre-wedding). The next two are of Theresa just being her usual ebullient self at the Scripps Ranch Fire Station. A few weeks prior a huge fire had burned through our community and destroyed hundreds of homes. Our home was preserved in large part because of the efforts of these and many other firemen. The fire burned within a half block of our home which had the old-style wood shingles which would have gone up in a minute.

Our neighborhood put together a feast and visited the fire station to thank all the firemen. Theresa as usual, had no problem asking handsome fire-men to pose with her for photos. And of course, she had to try on their firefighting equipment. All smiles and joy as always... bringing everyone into her vortex. God, how I loved to watch her at these times because in turn she brought immense joy into my life, and into the lives of everyone around her... A special gift that is to be treasured when you find it.

Comments (A sampling)

I remember the fire and how worried I was for you all. Theresa was soooo thankful that it didn't hit your home. – Lin M.

She was indeed a woman of joy. She embraced everyone with all that she was and with every memory we shared together, I am reminded of how she changed my life. I will always be grateful for her love and joy. – Sharon K.

• Life After First 6 Months and Holidays

Once I had experienced the full cycle of grief—deep grieving and my first trip through all the momentous days of the year—I began to find my "new normal." It did not happen suddenly, but it takes time; and, it will be different for each widower.

But you will recognize it when you:
- are not grieving as much every day, in fact you may have more and more moments of happiness or enjoyment;
- are going out more with new friends and groups;
- stop feeling so all alone all the time;
- are fine with staying home by yourself more;
- can think about a future without your spouse in it, such as plans for big trips; and,
- remembering your wife with fondness and gratitude rather than with sorrow and painful memories.

The following Caring Bridge Entries cover some of my thinking as I was working towards a healthier and happier place.

Caring Bridge #32: Life After the Holidays
By Fred Colby, January 13, 2015

The girls and I had our first taste of the holidays without Theresa, and it was not pretty. I felt like I was back in month one of the grieving process, with the full array of meltdowns and emotions.

Nothing can prepare you for this. All you can do is let the grieving to go on and try to know that you will come out on the other side at some point. I emerged from it all on New Year's Eve, and though there were still setbacks, they were not as severe.

Now I feel like I am restarting the recovery process as I realize that no one can ever replace Theresa. The most I can ever hope for is some new friends who can join me on this ongoing journey until it is time to rejoin my wife of 45 years.

As I continue to do research for my book on being a widower, it is not encouraging to find out that widowers are:

1. 300% more likely to die in a car accident

2. 400% more likely to commit suicide

3. 600% more likely to die of heart disease

4. 1000% more likely to die of a stroke

And widowers over the age of 75 have the highest rate of alcoholism in the country. So, looks like I have my work cut out for me if I want to stay healthy and alive a while longer.

Getting used to being alone after 47 years with the same wonderful loving woman is a real challenge. I understand why 52% of widowers remarry within 18 months, with over half of these marriages ending in divorce or abandonment. Losing a spouse is recognized as the most stressful event in one's life, one against which other stressors are measured.

In a sense, I felt as if I myself had died, as I lost such an important part of who I was. While men do seem to emerge from the grief earlier than women (with many reentering dating after 6 months while women will often wait for a year or two), the reality is that men do continue to grieve as much as women, just in a different way.

Men tend (as I have) to attack their grief through activities (see cleaning Theresa's stamp room, organizing photos, etc.), while women may retreat into more thinking, talking, going to groups, etc.

Men generally do not take advantage of the counseling help offered at hospices, churches and other locations unless encouraged by friends and family. I feel fortunate that I did turn to counseling two weeks after Theresa passed. It does not heal you, so much as help you keep a more level approach, to confront the emotions, to better understand what is going on, and to see that you are not going crazy.

The grief itself comes in waves, rather than in a steady progression up or down. You cannot anticipate it, as it may hit from out of nowhere. Fortunately, most breakdowns do occur when you are home alone, and you can just let it out. While in public the grieving can take more modulated forms from quiet tears to pausing while you regain your composure. The most others can do to help is to just realize that this is something we must go through and be supportive and loving as we try to deal with it.

I know that I and my daughters are extremely grateful to all of you who have been there for us as we try to cope with all the effects of grieving.

Thank you all, we love you.

Fred

- **Can I love again? And On Welcoming Death**

After a 45-year marriage to the love of my life it was difficult to imagine that I could ever love anyone again like I had loved her. Or, that I could ever love anyone again, period! I believed that I could make love, but not whether I could really get excited and care for someone else. Would I feel guilty? Would I be impotent? Would I say all the wrong things? The way that I found I could love again was both painful and hilarious in its own way. My therapist and I were literally laughing uncontrollably when discussing it.

The story begins with the following Caring Bridge entry.

Caring Bridge #26: From Grieving to Emergency Room to Home... Now What?

by Fred Colby, October 3, 2015

So, after surviving the first 3 months of this grieving process (though I still talk to Theresa every day) I went out with a friend for a beer and ended up in the emergency room having an emergency hernia operation a week ago. The experience had a profound effect on my grieving and healing process.

During the ordeal, I lost 10 lbs., made a bunch of new nurse friends, and gained a beard that the kiddos say to keep so we can see how it turns out. I spent a week at the hospital recovering, during which time I was so distracted that I did not think of Theresa or much of anything during the whole time.

For a time while going into surgery I thought maybe our reunification had just sped up a bit, and that I would be seeing her shortly. I even gave the DNR (Do not resuscitate) order, but for naught. The doctor asked me three times if DNR was in fact my choice. Sorry to say, I cannot report any near-death visitations or other magical moments that came out of all this.

My friend, Seth, was a trooper through all of it... driving me to the emergency room, sitting with me until I was admitted to the operating room, and talking by phone with my daughters to keep them informed as they rushed to get to the hospital.

Jen and Charlene were there every day helping me to get through this added challenge, and I am now home recovering at a pace which is guaranteed to drive me crazy within another week. It is kind of weird, cause my grieving which went into hibernation mode during the ordeal, kicked right back in where it left off after I got home... so no short cuts for me apparently.

I don't know what the heck the higher authorities have in mind for me now, but, apparently, I am not getting out of it, whatever it may be. No more clarity on that front than before... and trust me, you constantly ask yourself, God, and anyone who will listen to you... Why am I here now?? I understood my purpose clearly before all of this began, but that is all up for grabs now.... Except for one thing, I know I am still here to enjoy my great daughters and their families as much as I can before moving-on. Last week's little adventure just made it clear to me that death really can happen at any time.

Comments (a sampling)

Hang in there Fred. We all ask that question (I ask that ALOT now). We don't know how we may impact people along the way, in word or in deed. But you are a great grandfather to your little ones, and they have much to learn from you yet. — Linda P.

Here is the rest of the story I did not put on Caring Bridge

Shortly after leaving the hospital I returned to grieving for my wife as I had before entering the hospital. But about 4 days later a switch flipped in my mind, from "Grief On," to "Grief Off" just like a light switch. My depression lifted, and suddenly I was not grieving 24/7. I was beginning to think about me, my future, and what life might be like without Theresa being a physical part of it.

One of the consequences of all this and the anxiety that was building up over my future, was that I still was not sleeping well (three hours or less a night), my mind and body were still a wreck, delusions were increasing, and I was finding that I had erections for what seemed to be half of every day. I could not control any of it, and therefore I thought I was going crazy. I tried several methods to bring it all under control, but with no success.

About a week into this I had a dentist appointment for a regular checkup and cleaning. I told the dental hygienist about the loss of my wife, and she was immediately sympathetic.

I could see that she was having an emotional reaction and asked if she was going through something too. It turned out that she was getting a divorce and had a young son to take care of.

We totally bonded over the common grief and suffering we were going through, and by the time I left the office I was head over heels in love with this young and beautiful dental hygienist. I had no control over my emotions and knew that this was not going to work, but still was grateful to know that I could feel like that for someone again.

At this point I was literally out of control and knew I had to go see my therapist as soon as possible. When I met with her I described all my symptoms, including the stress, sleeplessness, delusions, erections, and falling in love with a beautiful dental hygienist half of my age. In describing all of this to her we realized how absurd much of it was and began laughing to the point of nearly rolling on the floor. (I do have a weird sense of humor, just in case you are wondering.)

After my own experience, I do believe that being willing to laugh at yourself is critical to surviving the grief.

When describing this I asked her, "What the hell is wrong with me? What can I do to get through this?" She advised that my body, mind, and emotions were telling me to get out there again and consider seeing other women. This sounded a little counter-intuitive as I was afraid to see any women while experiencing these symptoms. But after some reflection and looking at dating sites, I decided to post myself on a web site.

The outcome was that I was approached by a couple women on the web site and arranged my first non-wife date in 47 years. I purposefully choose someone who I knew sounded like a nice woman, but whom I was not particularly attracted to. I did this in the hopes that the erection issue could be kept to a minimum. The first date (over cheese and wine) went well, we had good conversations, I was more relaxed than I thought I would be, and the erection issue was kept to a minimum.

Building on this I went on a dating binge, having ten dates with eight different women over the next two weeks. With each date, my self-confidence increased, and my self-doubts decreased. (I was dealing not only with the age issue and time out of the dating scene, but also with a prosthesis that covered half of my nose due to surgery four years prior). The erection problem diminished with each date as well, to the point where it was a relatively minor problem. When I found a woman I really liked, it was no longer a problem (well, almost not a problem).

After talking to many widowers, I know others experience these same issues. After suffering what for most of us is the greatest loss of our life and feeling that we may never again have a woman who cares for us, it is almost intoxicating to find that not just one, but possibly many women are interested in meeting and engaging with you. With online dating, it is way too easy to end up with lots of dates that are never going to go anywhere.

I am convinced the constant erections were a reaction to these self-doubts, lack of confidence, and fear about the future. Unless you are an Adonis (and know it), very intelligent, have a fabulous sense of humor, and are comfortable in social settings, you probably have self-doubts, and your self-confidence may be shaky. I have yet to meet a widower who did not have self-doubts when re-entering the dating scene.

After being out of circulation many years and entering this strange new world of online dating services, it would be amazing if you were not insecure. Many of the women on these web sites are experienced pros when it comes to online dating, as the overwhelming majority of them are divorcees who have been in that situation for many years.

Another option is to join widow/widower groups, but these tend to be 80 to 95 percent women—a situation most men are uncomfortable walking into. There are also various 40+ and 50+ single groups which offer non-dating social activities through which you can meet women in friendly no-pressure situations.

Recommendation: If you find yourself in this condition, put yourself into non-sexual situations with women such as meeting over coffee or a glass of wine. Even lunch and dinner are okay if you don't press for or expect any intimate relationships. You will find that over time (in my case six dates) your situation improves with every date, and that eventually you will go on a date, enjoy a woman's company, and have no symptoms.

So, the key point is that **yes, you can love again**, you can meet nice women again, and you can get your physical, emotional and mental issues under control! But there will be ups and downs in part because of anxiety over your new relationships. Knowing that it will end is half of the battle.

- ## Learning to Live Alone – Truth or Bullshit?

As you redefine who you are, you find that you also must redefine how you relate to your wife even though she is now gone. She will never be absent from your life going forward, but neither will it ever be the same again, so you now must discover how she fits into your new life.

Sometimes, when people tell me that I must learn to be alone, they think that I want to remarry and have someone in my life 24/7. Nothing could be further from the truth. I am not trying to replace my wife with a new one. But, I am looking for companionship and yes, some love in my life, including physical intimacies with someone I really care for.

I agree that you should once again learn how to be comfortable by yourself, like when you were a young single male. I remember spending hours by myself just listening to music, watching a game, or working on the car—all without giving much thought to my "relationships" or girlfriends.

When I started dating after my wife's passing, I could think about little else but my new relationships. In hindsight, a year later, I can see that this obsession with other relationships was in large part about me trying to escape the grieving for my wife. I now know that it also had to do with the terrible insecurities that emerged along with the loss of self-identity. It was a challenge to learn how to spend an evening home by myself without dwelling on my loss, a new girlfriend, or other relationships.

I have noticed that most of the same people who say that I "need to learn to live alone" go out many times every week, maybe not with a partner, but at least with friends and family. So, they are not really by themselves. They are just not with a partner. There is a big distinction between being alone and being lonely.

I have never had a guy tell me that I needed to learn to live alone. It is always women who say this. Women are much more social than guys and have their networks to keep them engaged. Guys rarely have the same extensive networks, so they gravitate towards being out with a woman or being alone at home a lot more. Fortunately, I enjoy getting out with others, in groups and one on one. And, I enjoy the company of women, but can have fun out with the guys too.

When in an exclusive dating relationship with a close woman friend, I am perfectly happy being home alone for a few nights, even when apart for a week or so. Somehow, just having a special someone in my life gives me a calmness that allows me to better enjoy my time alone.

My warning here is to be cautious about what "advice" you take in as being a "truth" that dictates your actions and self-image. Don't be afraid to question accepted "truths" about the widower experience, even including what you read in this book. Each of us is different in our personal background, history, and culture. And so, each of us will experience things differently. We can learn from each other, but, need to be willing to blaze a different path if that is what helps us to get to a better place.

- ### Setbacks and Continuing Rollercoaster

One final warning: There are still setbacks you will experience as your rollercoaster ride continues, even after you have dispensed with the deep grieving. I progressed from hyper-emotional responses, to mid-range emotional responses, and finally to limited-emotional responses.

As the one-year anniversary of her death approached, I found my emotional responses to other women were going into a sort of hibernation. I could not emotionally engage with any woman. I think this was in part because I was mentally preparing for this milestone in my grieving process, and I was trying to figure out what my new relationship with my wife would be going forward. Until that was resolved, I did not see how I could really invest my heart and soul into any kind of new relationship.

- **Getting to a Healthier Happier Place**

The journey to becoming a new and more healthy, happy, secure and self-confident self is a convoluted and difficult one. Speaking from experience, you can do it if I did it. I am still working my way there, but after a year since my wife's passing, I can say that I am in a better place.

The challenges that confront you are overwhelming at first, but over time you will gain the confidence and drive to address the following categories and possibly more. The challenges I faced in order of importance to me were:

1. Meeting regularly with a therapist to confront mental health challenges. If you do not do this first, it is harder to address the other issues effectively.

2. Establishing a good exercise routine to achieve and maintain good physical and mental health, even if it is only going out for long walks each day.

3. Practicing prayer and meditation to help reduce stress in your body which can help reduce blood pressure, heart rate and respiration. Free meditation offerings can be found on the web to introduce you to the concept before seeking guidance to take it to another level. Many studies have shown the positive effect of meditation on improving your physical and mental health.

4. Learning how to do the things your wife may have taken care of, such as house cleaning. Pay someone if you cannot get yourself to do this. I found doing the chores was an effective way to keep myself active when home. Other items might include grocery shopping, paying the bills, monitoring family birthdays and sending presents, keeping everyone in the loop on family activities, and so on.

5. Finding activities, particularly group activities, where you can meet new people, hone your social and communication skills, and learn how to interact with women who might be of interest to you at some point. Locally I found a great 50+ singles Breakfast Club that was available via Meetup.com, a web site dedicated to connecting people together. Breakfast Club offered a wide array of activities like movies, meals, hikes, snow-

shoe treks, and game nights every week, so I could find at least one thing a week that appealed to me.

6. Establish new, reestablish old, and keep guy friends through getting together for a beer now and then. Your real friends will not be scared away by your up and down behavior, and they will be glad to be given a way to support you through your challenges. Like me, you may find that you must be the one to reach out to them. This is good practice for learning how to be the initiator of activities, rather than waiting for someone else to do it.

7. Branch out and try new things. Recognize that there are some activities you might not have tried during your marriage, places you might not have gone, books you might not have read, movies you might not have seen, and sports you might not have engaged in. For me this meant going out at night to many group activities, hiking, snowshoeing, digging deeper into topics like vulnerability, exploring spiritual philosophers such as Eckhart Tolle and Deepak Chopra, practicing meditation, and exploring yoga. You will find that new things will invigorate you, help to define your new self, and give you self-confidence to continue exploring new ways to grow as a person.

In *Widower: When Men Are Left Alone*, one widower remarked that his wife did not like camping or other outdoor activities that he enjoyed, so he lovingly stayed away from them. After losing her, he realized he didn't have to compromise. The desire he'd been sitting on for years could now be part of his new reality. He started getting together with friends to go camping, horseback riding, taking canoe trips, and going on bike rides.

The widower mentioned above found his way in part by joining a group of widows and widowers called LADOS (Life After the Death of a Spouse).

The Breakfast Club in Fort Collins was recommended to me by a widow friend of mine. There are groups all over the country, often listed on Meetup.com. When I felt ready to become active again, to meet new people, and to reengage with life, these groups were a lifesaver for me.

It was a little scary at first joining groups where I did not know a single person. However, I will tell you that as a guy I had a tremendous advantage as the women outnumbered the men by a factor of eight to one again. If you can hold you own in a group of women and not be afraid to suggest assorted topics more to your liking, you can really enjoy yourself.

The age range in the groups I joined were from 55 to 75. Over time I found which activities attracted the members I was most comfortable with. For example, the hikes and snowshoeing attracted a more active and somewhat younger crowd (55 to 65). And the game nights, brunches, lunches and dinners tended to attract a little older crowd (65 to 75). The more events that I attended, the more I became acquainted with the folks I enjoyed doing things with the most.

Gradually I developed real friendships with a few of the men and women in the groups. I built several platonic friendships with some of the women, and eventually found one gal who was really special. A few of the guys and I began to contact each other for a late afternoon Beer & Bull gathering where we could just shoot the bull like the old days.

I recommend that you just experiment and try different activities until you find a few that you really enjoy. Over time if you do end up dating one woman, you will find yourself torn between group activities and being just one-on-one with your new friend. The trick for my new friend and I was to find a balance between the two, which took time to figure out.

SECTION 3

AFTER DEEP GRIEVING

Chapter 7

It Will Never Be the Same Again

**Healing is active, not passive.
You must be actively involved in your own healing,
because time by itself will not heal all your wounds.**

One rude awakening I had as I began to have the semblance of a normal life again, was the realization that it would never be the same again. I believe that no matter what you do, no matter if or when you ever date again, no matter how busy you get with work and your social life, and no matter whether you marry again, it will never ever be the same again.

If like me, you had a very good or great marriage, you may never have that constant support, love, and connection again that you had with your wife. You may never have someone to talk with every day like you did with your wife. You may never have someone who can finish your sentences like your wife could. If you date again, you will probably find that things are very different when you only see each other two or three times a week instead of every morning and every night. I know I did.

I found out through research, friendships with other widowers, and my participation in various counseling groups that not every widower (and certainly not every widow) feels the need to find a new partner. For some, they are genuinely happy to continue as they are, to maintain their vows until their own death, and to honor their wife in this very tangible way. I have come to understand that it is not a betrayal to seek a new friend, nor is it a weakness to be content with remaining solo. We each must find the way which feels best for us.

I do not want to give the impression that you should reengage with women through dating again, or that you need to marry again. I honestly believe that many widowers are perfectly happy to emerge from their deep grieving without a need for this. However, studies do show that 52 percent of widowers remarry within eighteen months. From what I heard in conversations with other widowers, at least another 25 percent engage in dating again, mostly within a year if not sooner. That translates into roughly more than 75 percent of all widowers dating and/or remarrying within 18 months.

Whether you date again or not, I believe that every widower will find that he needs to have female companionship in his life again. This might be satisfied through family members, work mates, groups, or platonic friendships with women who are comfortable with this arrangement.

"Platonic" defined: I feel it necessary to define this term as I found some widowers took this to mean something very different than I did. A platonic relationship is a friendly, nonphysical, companionable, but sex free relationship. It is not one in which you and a new friend have sexual relations without any commitment or emotional attachment. You may find that this latter type of relationship could actually hinder your ability to become emotionally engaged with a woman again.

I found that many women just want to have a man in their life, but, not necessarily in a romantic way. Once I got past the "need" to have a romantic relationship, I could build several more platonic relationships with very attractive, intelligent, and fun women. This allowed me to get out, enjoy time with them, and learn how to build mature relations again. Over time, one of these may emerge as a much more meaningful relationship; but, I don't believe it must for me to be happy.

Recommendation: I cannot stress enough the need for you to slow down on making major decisions during the first year. My emotions, thoughts, self-image, and relationships changed dramatically during that first year. My thinking about key issues in the first six months was so different in the second year, in large part because I was a different person by then. Making decisions while your judgment is impaired is just asking for trouble, no matter how right your decision appears to be at the time.

Based on my experience, discussions with others, and what I have read, if you do marry again, I think you will find that things are just different. And I mean everything from how you are intimate with each other, to how you communicate with each other, to how you show affection for each other, and to how supportive you are of each other. Not to mention who does the dishes, laundry, and vacuuming.

I found that the more removed your partner is from her divorce or her husband's death, the more independent she is likely to be, and the more she will expect you to exhibit the same kind of independence.

I found that the women who are more communicative, more open to being with me all the time, and more generous with their time and affection would at times be too much for my taste. I found that they could be too clingy and too dependent upon me, to the point that I was uncomfortable with them.

Like me, you may find that at times you are the one being too clingy, too demanding of attention, and jealous of your new friend's time with others, such as their family and friends. This was a constant struggle for me during my early relationships. Many single women have spent years carefully building a protective cocoon of activities that fills the void for them. They are hesitant to part with any of it, for fear a new relationship will not work out and they will then have to rebuild their cocoon.

I was used to having a wife at home who made a point of speaking with me many times when I was absent, who emailed and texted me about everything from dinner to getting together with our family or friends. I was used to coming home and being greeted with love and affection, and to having conversations about our day. I missed this dearly and wanted the same with my new friends, but, it was not to be until a full year after my wife passed away.

When I entered an exclusive dating arrangement around seven months after my wife passed with a new friend, my expectations were unrealistic. I had to rein in my frustration over her failure (in my view) to respond to my phone or text messages in a timely manner, her lackadaisical (in my mind) approach to scheduling future dates and times to get together, and her prioritization of seeing her family and friends over me.

A lot of this frustration was in my own mind, and this caused me anxiety over the future of our relationship. She cared for me, rescheduled some things for me, she spent nights agonizing over our relationship, and made sure I knew that our relationship was important to her. And yet, I still felt frustrated. Why? Because it was different than the relationship I had with my wife during our many years together. I could not bring that feeling of total confidence and contentment back into my life.

I believe that this is one reason many widowers see remarriage as the one and only solution. They think that if they can just marry a woman and share a house, that they will then be able to recapture that feeling of love, support, and contentment that they had with their now deceased wife. I believe that the inability to recreate the prior marriage and all its benefits is a major reason why 50 percent of widower re-marriages fail. I have found that any good relationship takes work, real work! If a widower expects to find another woman, marry her, and then go right back into living the same way he did in his prior marriage, I believe he and his new wife are in for a very rude awakening.

Imagine the pressure you are putting upon the poor woman who marries you. All you ask of her is to recreate your former marriage and to make you happy! After reading a newspaper ad, "Looking for some-one to make me happy," philosopher Eckhart Tolle asks his audience, "Is that all?"

Think about it. Can someone else make you happy? Especially if you are already unhappy? Or do you have to become a more stable, content, self-confident, and happy person by yourself before you really connect with someone else? I believe that if you do this, you will have a much better chance of being able to find someone with whom you can develop a strong and stable relationship which can then add to your happiness and contentment. I found this to be proven true in my own experience.

The following Caring Bridge entry demonstrates some of what I was thinking on this topic during my post-deep grief process.

Caring Bridge #33: Contentment or Lack Thereof
By Fred Colby, January 15, 2016

As I sat in my recliner chair reading this morning, it struck me that what I miss most, now that Theresa is gone, is the sense of contentment that I had when she was here.

Like so many happily married couples, we did not need each other in the room to know that they loved, cared for, and would always be there for us.

I could be doing my thing downstairs while she was upstairs doing her thing. I did not need to talk to her, see her, or touch her to know that all was well. For most of our marriage, especially in the last 20+ years of it, we were both very content. Our lives were going well, we enjoyed each other, our family, our work, our community, and so on.

There was a real sense of contentment (I realize now how blessed we were to have this).

I remember thinking often or stopping to reflect, "Damn, I am so happy. I have a great life." I know from Theresa's frequent comments that she felt the same. I don't have that anymore.

I know that when I go out to the group activities or with new friends, that I am trying to regain that sense of contentment. What I get though, is temporary joy, or happiness in sharing activities, ideas, and support with each other. However, when I get home I still have that sense of loss, and that lack of contentment returns.

There is still a void in my life and I don't know if anyone can fill it for me. I realize I must be the driver to change my experience, if anyone can. Not too sure about the "how" right now. I am still searching on that one.

A new best friend might help me to get there, but I must be the catalyst in my change. Will anyone else ever love me the way that Theresa loved me? I don't know if that is possible. I believe it can help, it just won't be the whole solution. I must be an integral part of the solution if it is going to be real and long lasting. Then, hopefully, I can once again feel contentment! Wouldn't that be great?!!

Chapter 8

Building New Relationships

Success is stumbling from failure to failure with no loss of enthusiasm.
Source unknown; often attributed to Winston Churchill

We are built for relationships. The need for connection with others permeates the human body. Emotional bonding profoundly affects the mechanisms inside us that restore health and keep us healthy. The most powerful way to arouse those positive emotions that sustain health and healing is to connect intimately with another human being.
Trevor Crow and Maryann Karinch, from the Introduction to *Forging Healthy Connections*

Before we get into dating, let's first distinguish between dating to establish "relationships" and dating to have "affairs." As I have mentioned earlier, during your deep grieving cycle you may have an uncontrollable urge to be with a woman, sometimes within days of your wife's passing.

I can identify with one widower who says in *Widower: When Men are Left Alone*, that realizing his huge, almost obsessive desire to be with another woman led to an affair with a schoolteacher that he found "enormously cathartic. It made me feel like a whole man again."

His experience will not work for every widower, of course, and may even result in repercussions harmful to his healing process.

I know widowers who found themselves in torrid affairs within months of their wife's passing, and who subsequently had very painful ends to those affairs. They had not progressed in their grieving and found that they were still in the hyper-emotional stage which made their reaction to these breakups even more painful. Everything I have learned tells me that a woman who enters into an affair with a new widower who is still in the deep-grieving stage, runs an elevated risk of it ending painfully with serious repercussions for both parties.

To the woman who is becoming involved with a widower, be fore-warned that men who have recently experienced the loss of a wife may be clueless about what they are capable of. He may have such a strong desire to return to what used to be—or at least get away from things as they now are—that he can be unduly persuasive. If the woman wants to be persuaded, then an involvement could be a trap for both of them. His agenda could take them both down a treacherous path.

The opportunity to act on your obsession may not occur for every-one. Obsessed or not, once widowers emerge from the deep grieving stage I found that they are more likely to be interested in establishing real relationships, not just in having affairs. This was supported by my research and feedback I received from several widowers. Almost every widower I have met has spoken of the need to have a woman in their lives, even if only as a platonic friend.

Some were reluctant to engage in a romantic relationship, but, even these men wanted a woman to go to dinner with, to sit and talk with, to enjoy a movie with, and to take walks with.

This chapter is directed towards establishing relationships for those of you interested in finding a new best friend, not necessarily a new marriage partner. As discussed earlier, falling into a marriage too soon after losing your wife may have long term harmful consequences.

While dating may be the furthest thing from a widower's thought during the early months, and while he may even get angry when others bring up the topic, he may find that he needs to consider dating women as the best way to help pull him out of the constant focus on the loss of his wife.

I know that some may find the very idea of dating to be offensive during the first year after losing a wife. I found the constant focus on her and her passing to be depressing and unhealthy, though. The need to think about something else, another woman, does not mean that I did not love my wife and that I did not still think about her every day.

I found that before I started dating, it is best to resolve your new re-lationship with your wife. Many may tell you that your wedding vows said, "until death do you part;" not for eternity. The reality is that you will continue to have a relationship with your wife; it will just be a very different relationship.

From my own experience, and that of other widowers I know, I can tell you that your new partner or wife does not need to replace your first wife. If a possible new spouse forces you to choose, it can lead to friction and anger which can threaten the new relationship. Ideally there should be no competition between the new and old wife/partner. It may take a while, but you can find a way to accommodate the first wife without disrupting the relationship.

My belief is that, *for us to move forward, we need to know that we do not have to leave anyone behind.* As widowhood is much about the process of redefining yourself, so too it is about redefining the role of your wife in your new life. I had to figure out how I could continue to honor and love her, while at the same time making room in my heart and mind for new friends, and finally for a new girlfriend. This may take months or even years. It varies for each of us.

Much that I experienced validates everything that the authors of *Widower* reported. I was fortunate in that I dated a widow who recognized some of these symptoms and slowed things down until I could see what I was doing in terms of desperation, hyper-emotions, my need to persuade her, and the likelihood of failure in the relationship if we moved forward too fast.

I was also fortunate in my second relationship to have a woman in my life who was patient with me while we worked our way through to a good solid relationship. It took time, going home frustrated many nights, and a willingness to allow her to set the timetable for intimacy. This would help insure that by the time we mutually got "there," we would both be in a healthy place.

Eventually I met another woman for whom I was ready, both emotionally and mentally. I was in a much calmer place, and I had learned much about myself and what I was looking for in a new best friend through my dating experiences. This helped me better judge whether a friend was a good fit for a romantic relationship,

As previously discussed in Chapter 6, I found myself thrust back into the dating scene due to a strange series of events, including my emergency hernia operation, sleep deprivation, constant erections, and other symptoms which were resolved by engaging with women again.

I have heard from several widowers who went through very similar experiences and two who said they could have gone to bed with another woman within days of their wife's passing. After processing my own experience and the things that I learned through the dating process and research, I believe the symptoms have much to do with the widower's lack of self-confidence while entering his new world, as well as with desperation for a woman's touch and kindness. The sex act is just a physical manifestation of these other needs.

When I first started dating, I found that I had to overcome my self-doubts and lack of self-confidence. I was not the young stud I once was, and I really didn't have any idea of what to expect when I went out on my first date. While I was still in my hyper-emotional deep grief stage when I started dating, I did find that I could function well.

Warning on Imprinting and Signals: You may be familiar with the "imprinting" that baby birds, animals, and humans often have when first born. They will fix their attention on the "first object with which it has visual, auditory, or tactile experience and thereafter follows that object." (Source: Encyclopedia Britannica)

I believe that widowers often experience a similar bonding to the first viable woman who shows any interest in them and who shows them any kindness. My filters, or my ability to read signals from others, were all screwed up after Theresa's passing and I would have to constantly be on guard against misinterpretations of signals and imprinting upon women I met.

Like me, most of the widows and widowers I've met were married while still very young, many while still in their teens. I, and many of those I met, commented on how we felt like awkward teens once again as we reentered the dating scene—the same sweaty palms, qualms about how we look, and emotional ups and downs such as anxiety over what the date is thinking about us. It is scary and challenging. At times, I felt silly to feel these emotions again at my age, and I questioned myself about my sanity in reentering the dating world.

I learned to look at each date and relationship as a learning experience. I made mistakes, misinterpreted signals, and jumped to erroneous conclusions. The trick was to not act on any signals during my early dating experience, no matter how strongly I felt about it, and wait until my emotional state and self-confidence had stabilized.

Slow and steady brings real progress, while *fast and aggressive* may produce bad decisions and consequences.

I strongly recommend that you have a long and honest conversation with yourself about what kind of relationship you are seeking. Don't let your sex drive dominate your decision-making process. Allow yourself the time needed and multiple dates to help you eventually arrive at some clarity on this. If you are just looking for short term hookups, my advice will be of limited value to you. But, if you decide that you are looking for a strong healthy long-term relationship, then read on.

It is easy to make mistakes in the early going. I know of a widower who reached out within a week of his wife's death to an old high school flame who had lost her husband just six months previously. They met and married within three months.

The result was a disaster as the new husband reverted to old bad behaviors and his wife felt trapped in an unhealthy marriage. Everything I have learned says that widows and widowers are not emotionally or mentally prepared to make any major life decisions, much less marriage decisions, during the first six to twelve months. Due to the length of time widows tend to be in deep grief (one year or longer), they may be even less prepared to make marriage decisions during the first year or two. But no rule is absolute. I know of one case where a widow bonded with her husband's best friend soon after her husband's death, and remarried within a year, and it was successful.

I met and bonded with a two-year widow within a month of starting to date again, about five months after my wife's passing. We both re-acted in our hyper-emotional state and realized—her before me—that we were moving too fast and had to slow it down. Over time we real-ized that the relationship would not work due to her work schedule, family obligations, and her not being ready to make a real commitment to anyone at that time.

Get used to the idea that the women you date, if they are serious vi-able long-term options rather than short term hookups, may go through a series of push-pull reactions during your dates with them. By this I mean they will pull you in by allowing or encouraging hugging and kissing, and then push you away as they grow more fearful that things are moving too fast. So just go with the flow and let them dictate the pace until you get to a place where there is complete trust. This trust can support a more intimate relationship that has a chance of becoming long term.

I found it could be beneficial to the relationship to acknowledge this reaction by saying something like the following before they started to really pull away for fear of going too far, "I want you to know that I get it. Just because we kissed and hugged, I don't expect us to go into hyper-drive in our relationship now" or, "If you start to feel that things are moving too fast, just let me know." If you say something like this, her trust in you will grow exponentially and her relief may be visible. Take your time, allow the relationship to grow naturally and not forced by your sexual desire and emotional state.

I found that if you learn to take your time, you may be fortunate enough to not scare away that one new girlfriend who is just right for you. When I finally met one special gal, a widow for three years who had not dated since losing her husband, everything that I had learned before was invaluable to our establishing a good open loving relationship.

Now for some specific dating tips to help you get your head, your dating web site profile (if you go that way), and your dating etiquette in the right place so you can be successful.

The following advice is based on my firsthand experience derived from many dates with many women over the course of one year. I learned this during many ups and downs, and from conversations with widows and widowers as well as divorcees. Please remember that each of us may have very different experiences, so as you read the following take what you can from it that you think will work for you.

- ## Dating Tips for Widowers

a. Be yourself: You will need time to find out who you are now. You have changed and will continue changing! Take your time, talk to lots of people, try new things. For me, examples of this were snowshoeing, dancing, and going to movies with groups. Allow time to explore who this new you is, and don't be afraid to ask for help. This does not mean to become unhinged from your core values and beliefs, but it does mean that you may find that you are more adventurous now, more willing to accept others into your life, more empathetic towards others, and less fearful of challenges.

b.   Start a list, which will change over time: What kind of woman do you want in your life? What don't you want in your new friend? Do not expect to know what you want in your life right away. What you wanted 30, 40, 50 or more years ago, is probably very different from what you want now in a relationship. When we were young, physical attraction was such a major part of what drove our early relationships. As we mature we look for other qualities as well.

c.   Not the same woman: Don't just go out looking for a duplicate of the woman you lost. If that is your main criterion you may be very disappointed. You have changed, women have changed, and your comfort zone may change as you meet more women. You may find that you want women who are more active than your wife was, who want to travel more than your wife did, who want to go to plays more than you wife did, and so on. If you try to duplicate your past wife, you may not see that special woman who is right in front of you. I can pretty much guarantee that you will find women are much more independent and stronger now. Also, I found that my first impressions of the women I dated were more subject to change as I got to know them better. I found that a woman with many good attributes would become more and more attractive to me in other ways, including physical, as well. When I was much younger, these first impressions usually stuck and did not change.

d.   Many dates and many women: Plan on dating many women, even if you find the "right" one early in the process. This is important because you will find that you need to rediscover what you are looking for in a woman. It may well be different. Each woman you meet will have different qualities and interests. As you meet and get to know them certain qualities and interests may rise in importance to you. I found that finding a woman who really "got" me and my unique sense of humor was important.

Also, I found that conversation had become very important

to me, so the women who could really carry their side of the discussion rose in my estimation. You will likely find that your attraction to certain women may change as you come to appreciate various aspects of their bodies and behaviors. Dating many different women will help you to make better decisions when choosing your new best friend.

e. Barriers: One thing that has changed a lot since our younger dating days, is the number of barriers we have all built up over the years. Some of these barriers are "protections" we have developed to keep ourselves from harm, others are developed to insulate us from uncomfortable discussions or decisions. These may not be obvious at first, on either side. Barriers can include such conscious or unconscious practices as unwillingness to trust others, talk openly, share one's dreams or desires, explore new experiences, or discuss physical limitations.

   I found that I needed to be honest about my own barriers and to decide if I wanted to overcome them. If the answer was, "Yes," I had to decide how to best overcome them. Also, I found that over time I could identify my date's barriers and then sometimes find a way to discuss or address these barriers. Some, such as trust, are only overcome over time as you earn that trust. Some are insurmountable and will kill any chance of having a healthy relationship. When you find a partner, who has very few barriers, say hallelujah.

f. Opposites vs. Similarities: Opposites often attract when we are young and looking to find someone who completes us, as we are still relatively undeveloped human beings. As an older more mature adult I found myself being attracted to women who were more like me. Based on conversations with therapists and research, we do this in part because we feel more complete in our more mature state, and, we may now prefer compatibility rather than the challenge of a multi-year growing experience with a new mate. During my first meaningful relationship, my new gal friend and I were both surprised by how much we had in common. I was surprised by this and had to conduct research to convince myself that this was okay. I found out that not only was it okay, but, that it was the norm as we grow older.

g. Be open and honest: Many women seem to have an intuitive gift for detecting deceit or lies for what they are, often very quickly. And then you will have lost all opportunity to engage them in an honest and meaningful way. If you have something (in my case a partial nose prosthetic) that you believe might surprise a date or turn them off, be open and up front about it. I put this in my dating web site profile and photo, so I knew that any women who went out with me were not put off by it. The classic story is of Dr. Michael Burry (of *The Big Short* fame), who in his Match.com profile, described himself frankly as "a medical resident with only one eye, an awkward social manner, and $145,000 in student loans." He met and married a beautiful woman who loved his honesty.

If you have trouble being open and vulnerable, consider watching Dr. Brené Brown's 2010 TEDtalk on "The Power of Vulnerability." In our changing world, vulnerability is often no longer seen as a weakness, but, rather as strength. It shows an ability to be honest both with yourself and others. It allows us to confront our issues in a way which makes us stronger.

If you find it difficult to talk to women, if you wait for them to lead every discussion, and if you clam up when personal topics come up you are likely to have as much trouble communicating with women as the geeks on television's hit show *The Big Bang Theory*. I found that learning how to be open and have real conversations is attractive to women and helps you to confront issues that need to be talked about. It helps you to find those issues that would keep you from becoming a serious couple.

The tendency when you first start to date may be to try to please your date by saying what you think she wants to hear. This can lead to glossing over some obvious differences. I learned quickly that it was better to find out if you are incompatible early on, rather than finding out later in the relationship. Being open, honest and communicative can help you to avoid wasting time on women who are not your match, and to have more time to find the one who is your perfect match. I found it necessary to find a balance between being open and over-talking or over-analyzing things.

h. Get your priorities straight: If all you are looking for is sex, you will probably be sorely disappointed, or perhaps end up in a situation that you will later regret. Make a commitment to yourself to not even discuss that topic at all during the first few dates, even if the woman brings it up. This is a Catch 22 where just about any comment you make can and will be used against you. If she raises the topic, it is usually indirectly. You will find that each woman and each situation is different. Don't be afraid to slow things down, even saying sex is not a priority at this point, that you want to get to know each other better first. This helps to alleviate the pressure until you are both ready. With the right woman, the topic will come up naturally when you are both ready.

i. Sexually Transmitted Diseases (STDs): I hate to throw this out there, but STD is a huge problem in the older population, with rampant problems in retirement complexes. To avert some of the most serious problems, there has been a major effort to provide both men and women in these retirement settings with the HPV vaccine; don't be afraid to ask about whether or not your partner has had the vaccine. Be alert; know with whom you are going to bed and whether or not she has other sexual partners. Come prepared with condoms. Within reason, you will find that the women you date will often be open about when and if they have had other "serious" relationships. They will expect the same honesty from you. Many of us grew up sexually in a time when most STDs were easily curable; times changed with the intrusion of infections that are, perhaps, treat-able and controllable, but not curable.

j. Organic Dates vs. Website Dates: I dated several women who I met through web sites, and others I met organically (through old friends or activities). The website dating process can be expensive and exhausting, with many one or two date scenarios which lead nowhere. Organic dates can start from a healthier and more open place, as both of you know each other before the first date. At least you have an idea of what that person is like.

I met, dated, built extended relations, and then ended relations with two very nice women I met through website dating sites. After the second one ended I decided to go entirely organic and only date women who I had known or met recently. These dates were a lot less pressure filled and comfortable in the early going. Eventually I did meet a wonderful woman this way.

So, I encourage you to go organic if you already have women friends you can date without risking the loss of great friendships. If you do not have a go to circle of women friends, the website option can work well for you. But, as you will see below, it is real work!

k. Dating sites: Dating web sites are prolific, and often have very specific focuses based upon age, faith, ethnicity, orientation, and even new age spirituality. The tried and true Match.com is still out front in many ways, having the most registered users. OurTime runs a close second for those of us over 50, while eharmony, MeetMindful, Zoosk, Elite Singles, Plenty of Fish, Chemistry and others compete for your business. Some cross-advertise on each other's web sites, knowing that you might want to reach more women. After researching and then experimenting with Match, OurTime, Chemistry, and MeetMindful, I found that Match.com still produced the most matches for me. My conclusion was that a "nice guy" has a good chance of finding several women to date on any good dating site. Players and those seeking a fling are numerous. If you do your profile right, you will attract women seeking to avoid the "players."

l. Avoiding dating site scams: Once you've completed your profile—and do not share information on it that can be used to scam you such as birth date or address—you will find that you are approached at least daily by pretty young women (usually with a selfie showing a little cleavage) who are trying to get you to text, call, or email them directly rather than through the web site. Hit "delete" mentally and literally and move on. For all you know, these "hot babes" may be a fat, hairy guy sitting in his shorts sending out these tempting messages designed to take advantage of you while you are most vulnerable.

m. Using dating sites to choose well: When you first join, you will be overwhelmed by the variety of women on the site and have trouble knowing which ones to try to contact. Know that photos do not always do them justice, while some women will spend hundreds of dollars to have professional photos taken just for the web sites. Some pay others to write their biography. Try to see past all the posed images and old photos to find the real woman behind the profile. Don't be surprised when you first meet some of the women and find out that they do not look at all like their photos (you may not either). Many women can have a beautiful face while their bodies are not what they represent online.

My preference was someone who could communicate well, as that let me know that we might have good conversations, so we could build a real relationship. I was particularly drawn to women who demonstrated a sense of humor, who could laugh at themselves, and who said they liked to do things like laugh out loud while dancing in the supermarket aisle.

Be realistic. If a woman presents herself as an "extreme athlete type", and this is not your thing, don't waste your time trying to build a relationship with them. Stick to ones who have common interests, or at least interests you want to develop.

n. What you put into a dating site is what you will get out of it. To have a successful experience you need to:
  • Put real thought and effort into your online profile.
  • Choose good photos that express who you are, including ones that show you can really laugh, and laugh at yourself

as well. Include about four to eight non-staged photos.

- Respond honestly to as many of the web site questions as you can.
- You may see this differently, but I recommend setting the age range you are interested dating from about eight years your junior up to two years older than you.
- You will get fraudulent "favorites" or "flirts" from some 20+ years younger women from all over the country almost daily. Delete these and do not respond to them. You can notify the web site provider and they can often reduce the number of these you get.
- Don't waste time on the women who are not your cup of tea just because they look good—yes, the super athletic toned women did appeal to me, but their intense focus on the body was not what I was looking for. There are enough who are up your alley, focus on them.
- Looking and responding to constant emails from the dating sites can be addictive. Learn to block off specific times to respond to them rather than responding immediately every time you get one.
- Be responsive to those who reach out to you; most, if not all, are putting themselves out there just like you are, so be courteous and kind. For women from outside your geographic boundaries, just say you have decided to stay closer to home. It is hard enough to develop a good relationship with someone within a half-hour drive. I found it very difficult to do so with someone much further away.
- Know that some of the women are just lonely and just want a guy to talk to. Sometimes, you need to find a polite way to say thank you but no thank you.
- Reach out daily to at least one new woman until you are talking to as many as you are comfortable with. Your outreach can prompt her to look at your profile. If interested, she will let you know. Non-responsiveness often indicates non-interest, but it might just mean she is taking a brief hiatus or is focused on her work, family, or other interests.
- Try to establish a little dialogue with a woman before you

meet her. This builds a bit of a rapport that makes the first meeting less awkward, more like friends meeting.

- Know that numbers favor the "nice guys," as the number of women in the field tend to vastly outnumber the guys. So be prepared to respond sometimes to several new women in a day. As you build a list of possible prospects, you may communicate with four or five a day. It becomes real "work," not to mention the ongoing work of building relationships once you meet a woman or women that you like.

- Use photos that show you for who you really are. Not outdated photos from ten years ago or shirtless photos—unless you really are a sportsman type guy and that is the type of woman you want to attract. And, please, no touched-up photos. Feel free to show one or two with grandchildren because they humanize you and help to communicate your story. Also, I like to use one old photo in your younger days, such as a high school yearbook photo, with it clearly marked as such and with a little humor ("So I cheated with a photo from my surfer boy days").

- If you are a quiet guy, say so. If you laugh out loud, say so. If you are a jeans type guy, say so. If you want sophisticated, say so. Be totally honest and you are much more likely to attract the women who are the best fit for you. You find out very quickly that when you date a mismatch the relationship goes nowhere.

- Changing norms of dating sites: You will find that courting a woman online can in some ways be similar to your past experiences, and in other ways completely different. The women who have been on the web site for a while are well versed in the new game of communication, while the new ones will be just learning it like you are.

- "Nurse or Purse": You will hear this expression repeatedly. Women say that most men on the site are looking for a nurse, that is, someone to take care of them in ill health, or a purse—someone to help them become financially solvent. So, in your profile try to communicate to them if you are healthy and financially independent. Be honest, please.

Don't get too specific, but you can show a photo of you hiking or skiing, and maybe talk about a recent or planned trip to address these issues effectively but indirectly.

- Risks: Of course, you should be aware that there are also many "needy" women looking for a nurse or a purse as well. So be on guard. Don't over-share. Wait until you have had a couple dates at least before you even give a glimpse into your finances. I found it common for both me and my date to share some information about our situation, without getting too specific.

- Truth and Trust: If you stretch the truth about your health or financial situation don't expect to develop a healthy long-term relationship. If you think trust was important when you were twenty-one, I can tell you it is the single most important element in building relationships at a later age. Divorcees often come into the date suspicious by nature, while widows are particularly wary about this new experience and hesitant to move forward at all. The widows are usually more removed time-wise from the loss of their spouse, and often unsure about their decision to enter the dating game. They are likely to bolt at the first sign of deceit, as they should.

o. Responding to dating –site opportunities: First Contact: I found that sending a "Favorite" message or commenting on a photo in a humorous or specific way works well. She will then look at your profile, and if interested will send you an indicator that she might enjoy talking to you some more. Reach out to just a few to start until you get some responses and learn how to communicate with them effectively.

   You may find a few women, especially when you are new to the web site, reaching out to you through similar techniques. I found that getting a back and forth conversation going via email helped you to get to know each other a little before meeting. This reduces the anxiety over a first face-to-face meeting.

- Emails: Before you send a full email response to a woman, bring up her profile on a separate tab so you can refer to it while writing your email to her. Try to address specific things in her profile, such as background, trips referenced, or things she is looking for in a new friend. Point out things you have in common, or things you especially agree with. This will show that you did read her profile, rather than just looked at her photos. Conduct a real conversation.

- Smart, attractive and independent women: Due in part to their own lack of self-confidence, widowers may have trouble approaching women who come across in their profiles as being smarter (PhD), more self-assured, and more independent. Even though they have a PhD these women often indicate a willingness to date guys with less education. Don't let them scare you off. If one of them appeals to you, they will appreciate a genuine interest and conversation. Many guys fear them, but, these women are usually open to meeting and dating guys of all backgrounds. They often are just looking for men who are open, honest, and can carry an enjoyable conversation without blowing smoke to try and impress them. Because many of these women receive few viable matches, they can be even more appreciative of the guy who approaches them with openness, honesty, and a little humor.

- Emails before meeting: There are no guidelines on how many you should exchange. It will vary from woman to woman. I recommend at least three email exchanges before proposing a meeting. Some will want to carry on an extensive email exchange before being receptive to a meeting. Allow the woman to set the time and place to make her feel at ease and safe. If she is hesitating to suggest places, offer a few different options for her to choose from.

- Texting: I usually would not give out my phone number for texting unless I had a good feeling about the woman I was communicating with. Once you have given out your number, she can contact you at any time, and you might find this intrusive. At times, I was conducting texting conversations with up to three women at night. Be careful to not send the wrong message to the wrong woman! I did this more than once, and even sent messages intended for a girlfriend to my daughters by accident.

- Phone conversations: Some women, particularly those who live further away, will prefer a phone conversation with you before meeting you. This helps them to determine if you can really carry a conversation, and whether you sound like someone they would like to share a cup of coffee or glass of wine with. Allow enough time, perhaps up to an hour or more, to have a real conversation. Many men, like me, are not used to carrying on a phone conversation of over ten minutes. If you are not comfortable at first, prepare a list of questions to work from, such as:
  - o What book are you reading now?
  - o What movie would you want to go see?
  - o Tell me about your family. How close are they to you?
  - o What trip would you want to take if you could take any trip you wanted?
  - o And questions that work off their profile.
- Stalkers: Yes, women can be stalkers too. This is one great reason to keep your communications via the web site rather than direct or through phones. It can be quite touchy trying to let a "stalker" down gently in a way that she gets the message but is not hurt.

p. Dating etiquette: While times have changed, and women are much more independent these days, they still expect you to behave well during your dates. Nothing can turn a woman off faster than your bad behavior on the first date. Over time she may learn to tolerate some unruly behavior, but, you won't get this opportunity if you do not survive the first two or three dates. Does this mean you should be someone that you are not? No, but you should put yourself into their shoes and think about how your behavior might be perceived by them. You may only get one chance at getting to know Ms. Right, so don't blow it by raising red flags all over the place. It is hard enough to get to a second date with good behavior. Bad behaviors pretty much guarantee that you will not get there.

Adhere to basic good behaviors, such as:

- Dress appropriately for your area. This may mean jeans in one community, and slacks and sport shirt in another.
- Arrive a few minutes early, and then wait outside near the entrance where she can easily spot you.
- When she arrives, stand up and smile and welcome her with her name and a "friend" type hug, not too close or personal. Occasionally a woman may offer her hand for a handshake first to avoid the hug, but I found almost all are okay with a first "friend" hug.
- Hold the door open for her and if getting a beverage, go first and offer to pay. Some will insist on paying their share, let them do so if they are insistent. Nothing turns a woman off faster than the guy who won't even spring for a cup of coffee, however, there are some who want to demonstrate that they can pay their share and/or don't want to be obligated in any way on a first date.
- Pay attention, listen and respond to conversational leads. Don't just sit back and let her carry the whole conversation. Women are usually turned off by the guy who cannot converse with them.
- Be totally open and honest, be vulnerable. Don't conceal everything. As a widower, I can tell you that your "filters" —those psychological markers that tell you what is appropriate and what is not—may need calibration. For example, on early dates, I would often bring up going away on a trip together way too soon. This takes time, and you may unintentionally say some things that are inappropriate. When this happens, just own it and hope they can move beyond it. Apologize if something that you said was suggestive or inappropriate in some way. You will learn by doing, as will your new friend if she is willing to grow with you. If she easily takes offense and cannot move beyond it, she may not be the right woman for you anyway.

Avoid the following bad behaviors:

- Suggestive remarks
- Critical remarks about her appearance or behavior

- Crude jokes, rude noises, or cussing of any kind
- Dressing shabbily with no concern about the impression you make
- Sitting too close or touching her inappropriately
- Getting your coffee/wine before they arrive
- Checking your watch like you have somewhere else to be

q. Dating younger women: By younger I am referring to those who are around eight to fifteen years your junior, not the super younger women. I found that quite a few women who were about ten years younger would reach out to me, or they would respond to my inquiries. Most did not think it was a big deal but be aware of the "purse" as being a possible driver. Also, several that I met were surprised how busy I was and appeared to want an older guy who was not busy and who would be always available to them. Also, I noted that most if not all of them were working full-time and lived in apartments or shared living arrangements. This suggested that they were not financially set and may be looking for a guy with sufficient funds to take care of them later in life. So, just be aware as you enter these relationships.

r. Dating pledge: After hearing several horror stories about web site dating from a few of the women I met, I put a "Dating Pledge" at the bottom of my online profile. It goes as follows:
   1. I will always treat you with respect
   2. I will ask you to suggest our early meeting places, where you feel safe.
   3. I will never make suggestive remarks to you (at least not until you want me to).
   4. If we get there, YOU, not I, will decide when we can advance in our relationship.
   5. I understand that building relationships can take time, even when there is that early spark.

s. Starting over and over: I had to learn the hard way, that even when you find someone who you click with, you may find yourself back at square one more than a couple times. Try to date several women, identify one or two you enjoy going out with, and then narrow it down to one you want to get serious about. Then, it becomes important for both of you to demonstrate good faith by not dating others until you both decide whether this is in fact a meaningful relationship. This should be an open conversation.

Warning: This is also the time that you both start to really analyze the relationship and what it means to you. This is the time you begin to ask yourself, "Do I really care for her? Is this love? Or can this turn into love? Would I be happy spending an extended amount of time with her?"

You might want to experiment by allowing yourself to spend real time apart such as when one of you takes a trip or spending serious time together such as two days in the mountains or at a beach. The scenario is separate beds if you are not at the point of sharing a bed yet. But here's a warning: This is hard to do even with the best of intentions. This will force you to really think about how you feel about missing this new woman in your life? Do you miss her? Does she miss you? Do we run out of things to talk about when we are together for extended periods? How does that feel? How common are your interests?

The other test comes when you commit to having frequent dates. Your new friend may have been single for a lot longer than you have, and she has probably become an expert at filling every spare moment of her day with family, work, friends, and community activities, in part to fill the void of loneliness left by her divorce or widowhood. Alternately, she may just have learned to really value her "alone" time.

You may have become active yourself. I joined two boards, worked on this book, participated in group activities, and went to some activities with friends. When you both make a commitment to see each other two or three times a week, you will find, as I did, that this is more difficult than you ever thought possible. You will both be forced to decide whether you want to forgo some of those other activities to spend serious time with each other. If there is a wavering in this commitment, one or both of you may not be ready for a committed relationship or just not feel strongly enough to forgo those activities.

t. Dealing with anxiety: It is only natural that as you enter more serious relationships that you will begin to experience anxiety about your new friendships. This will be much more pronounced than worrying about how you look, whether you said the wrong thing, or offended a date somehow. You will now be really invested in a relationship and your concern over blowing it up can become obsessive to the point of setting your recovery from grief back a few months. I found that I was worrying about my new relations so much that I was having trouble sleeping, getting things done, and making good decisions. The need for sleeping aids became more pronounced again. If you can recognize this anxiety for what it is and confront it before it ruins your relationships, you will be way ahead of the game.

Rather than turn to prescription drugs, which I try to avoid like the plague, I turned to a religious philosopher named Eckhart Tolle. What appealed to me was his advice for getting out of worrying about the future or being depressed about the past, by focusing on the present. His message is simple, and follows the famous quote by philosopher, Lao Tzu: "If you are depressed, you are living in the past. If you are anxious, you are living in the future. If you are at peace, you are living in the present." Go to YouTube and search for "Eckhart Tolle and Anxiety," you will find several talks there which can help you. Tolle is an intriguing character with a funny laugh and way of speaking, but his messages often go to the core of feeling and thinking.

u. Intimacies different now: If like me you were old-school in terms of your intimacies with your wife, I have news for you: It may be very different for you in your new relationship. Once that big decision is made to cross the Rubicon and engage in sexual relations, it can be a real revelation. I heard this from several women before I reached this point, so I was not quite so surprised as I might have been. I found it more open, much more directed towards pleasing each other, and more work and play! In some vital ways, this is much more physically enjoyable for both.

At first, I found that thoughts of my wife, about my performance, and all kinds of others worries would invade my thinking while engaging in the act. I was surprised to find that "guilt" was not a major factor, but, just thinking about her was a factor. You may be affected several ways, including but not limited to: inability to achieve erection, delayed ejaculation (that is, long intimacies that may or may not result in ejaculation), laughter about unexpected and new experiences, questioning what is not working the way it did when you were with your wife, and much more. In addition to your thoughts, you may need to consider how stress, alcohol, food intake, exercise, and other mental health factors affect your performance.

My advice is to not dwell on it. Don't let a poor performance get to you, because "poor performance" is meaningless if your heart is in the right place. Let things take their natural course. If you have a partner who really enjoys you as a person, you will figure it all out. Overemphasis on performance is useless and will only make things worse.

v.   What to do if you find Ms Right—no quick decisions: You will probably date several, if not many, women before you find that special one who not only lights your fire, but just feels right in so many other ways. If you just rely upon physical attraction as the indicator, you may well be disappointed soon thereafter. I purposefully learned to slow things down a little bit when a new woman and I both began to get more serious about where we were going. I really wanted to make sure that our relationship was built upon a more secure foundation, one that would last a long time. I did not want to mislead a woman just to get into the sack with her, and then break it off shortly thereafter because there was nothing solid in the relationship.

For this reason, after you've survived several dates, I highly recommend talking things through with your new best friend and mutually deciding how best to proceed. This might include stepping back a bit, slowing things down a little, or even seeing what some time apart feels like. This is often a time of turmoil for the woman as she struggles with the decision about having a more intimate relationship and making that emotional commitment to you.

You should allow her some space to process her feelings. If you push too hard too fast, there is a good chance you will drive her away from you. However, when you meet Ms. Right don't be surprised if a spontaneous mutual decision to advance your relationship occurs.

The decision you both make after allowing enough time to process everything is much more likely to be one you can both live with for a long time, and one you are less likely to regret.

There are no guarantees no matter what you decide, but, the more you do to insure a good decision the more likely you are to be happy with it.

You may find, as I did, that a new relationship is both very familiar in some ways, and very different in other ways. Instead of dating women who looked just like my wife, I found I was meeting women who were quite different in terms of physical appearance, background, and cultural origins.

I discovered that I was attracted to women who were like my wife in terms of their values, their treatment of others, their loyalty to friends, and their disposition when faced with challenges. In other words, who they were as a person had become of primary importance to me, and the best indicator of whether we could build a long term and successful relationship.

I found that the best new relationships I had were ones where my new friend and I just felt comfortable with each other. I confirmed that this feeling of "being comfortable" was also one cited by other widowers who had entered long term relationships after their deep grieving period had ended.

Chapter 9

Sharing Your Life with Two Women

Not all of us will choose to move forward with new relationships. For some of us, it will be too painful to let go of your wife and to replace her with a new friend. But for many, it is more of a question of when and how to move forward with new relationships. My message is that you can still have your wife in your life and have a new friend, that you don't have to completely "let go" of her and your memories.

This chapter is directed to those widowers who choose to move forward with a new relationship, whether through marriage or simply being with someone new on an extended basis. No one way—new relationship or remaining devoted to your deceased wife—is right or wrong. Only you can decide what is right for you.

One thing you will need to prepare yourself for, if you develop a serious relationship with a new woman, is the idea that you now have two women in your life. Your new friend will never totally displace your wife. If she attempts to do so this may ruin any chance that you have for a long term successful relationship.

However, it is imperative that you first, and her second, learn how to live with your wife still occupying a place in your heart and your thoughts. While you may no longer have daily grieving for your wife, you will still have moments of grieving probably for the rest of your life. In fact, you will likely continue to have occasional deep grieving regressions such as around holidays or anniversaries. The sooner you come to terms with this, the sooner you can find a way to work around these issues without destroying your new friendship.

Around the tenth month after my wife's passing and five months of dating I got to that place where I realized the need to figure out how my wife fit into my life going forward. Prior to this I swung between the extremes of thinking of her in the old ways, or of displacing her from my thoughts with thoughts about my new best friend. Neither approach was really working.

Around the tenth month, I started to become more balanced in my approach. I still thought of her early in the morning and late at night, and allowed thoughts about her to weave their way into my day more naturally, rather than dwelling on her for extended periods. I could cut back the number of times I was referring to her when with others, and to not agonize over the status of my relationship with her so much. I could do this while not in any intense relationships with other women.

Interestingly, as my thoughts about her became more balanced and my stress over her absence reduced, I could see her in my dreams more. I still cannot visualize her in my thoughts. I am interested to see if my ability to see her continues to evolve as our new relationship develops.

As I came to realize, accepting a new friendship into your life does not mean you must leave an old one behind. Part of the process of building your new friendship will be to talk openly about this, and to be considerate of your new friend's feelings as well. This may mean accommodations such as:

- Removing your wife's clothing from the master closet, and perhaps the house.
- Putting your wife's ashes away into a less used room or taking them out and spreading them somewhere appropriate.
- Reducing the number of photos of her in your home except in places like your office or her hobby room.
- Gradually reducing the number of references to your wife in conversations with your new friend until they are minimal.
- Letting her know when you are having a return to grieving, so your new friend can give you some space, and hopefully even understanding and supporting you as well.

Regret – Guilt and Late Messages from Your Wife: Once I entered a loving relationship with another woman, my thinking was that I had little or no guilt or regrets about the new relationship. However, six weeks into it, I suddenly had a rather intense and meaningful dream which suggested otherwise.

In my dream, my wife was interacting with me and the family in a past home. While everything seemed normal in our relationship she told me that she wanted a divorce. Since we had never had occasion to have such a conversation in our marriage this was a bit of a shock, even in the dream. We were still discussing it when I awoke from the dream.

It occurred to me that the meaning of the dream was that she was, in my mind at least, somehow aware of the new relationship and letting me know that this might mean some sort of separation for us going forward. To me this indicated that I did in fact have some guilt or reservations about the new relationship and the intimacies that went with it. This spurred a reevaluation of how I was thinking about my new friend and a willingness to confront this deep-seated regret or guilt.

I did not want to give up my wife and our long relationship, and neither did I want to give up my new relationship. I am not sure how I will resolve this, but now I am aware that at a subconscious level I am facing some new questions and challenges that must be addressed.

Other widowers I spoke with have said they've had occasional struggles with subconscious thoughts invading the bedroom as well. If you are fortunate, as I was, your new gal friend will be patient as you work this out. I found it better to be open with my new friend about what I was going through, including the dream. We both knew that this was probably a short-term thing which would dissipate over time.

Patience in Building Your New Relationships: Regardless of your personal experience, you may find you and your new friend are facing challenges that had not occurred to you before, such as how to introduce the families of you and your new friend to each other. One of the greatest fears I had was that my daughters, brothers, sisters and friends would not welcome my new friend into our family. I know that my new friend had the same fears.

Like one couple (a widow and widower) I know of, you might have to be patient and wait until the right time to introduce each other to your respective families. This can be difficult, as you may be ready to take the relationship to the next level (be it intimacy or marriage), but feel the time is not right yet. If you have long established old school morals, you may fear others will condemn you for "living in sin" or for betraying your wife's memory.

If you are patient and take the time to properly introduce everyone to each other, and to building solid ties between the families, you may find the next steps occur naturally and with the full approval of your children, brothers, sisters and friends. This can bring blessings as you can now be surrounded by an extended family which makes your life even fuller and more enjoyable.

When I met my new friend, we had a couple of dates before taking a long walk around a park in the Fort Collins area. As we approached the parking lot a car pulled up beside us and I heard young children in the backseat yelling "Popa." It was my daughter and two granddaughters. My friend looked and said in wonderment, "Charlene? Is that you? Ceci, is that you?" It turns out that my new friend, knew both of my daughters and had met all my grandchildren through an area preschool.

We found that I had already met one of her daughters and grandchildren as well. This familiarity definitely made it easier on us as our relationship developed. We built on this by including each other in our family events, and then later by joining each other on family trips. Over time our family and friends warmly accepted us into their circles. We know that if and when we decide to make our relationship more formalized in some way, that this foundation will make that much more acceptable for everyone we care for.

The point is pretty simple, like me you may need to slow things down occasionally to consider all the implications for you, your new friend, and your families. If you take the time to do things right, you are likely to receive many more blessings down the road.

Post-Script 18 Months After Wife's Passing

I am happy to report that the guilt and doubts about "leaving" my wife for my new best friend gradually diminished over the next year and I could enjoy the new relationship fully. This does not mean that I don't have occasional doubts and regrets, I do; but, their predominance in my thought and dreams has gradually diminished to the point where they no longer cause me pain or misgivings.

In some ways I think this was made possible because my new friend was a widow. Our common experience allowed us to support each other in our need to remember and honor our former spouse.

To my fellow widowers, and to those who love them, my message is to not give up on a healing process that comes naturally if you will allow it into your life. Be open, be receptive, and most of all learn to be grateful for the good you have already received; then, and only then can you be ready to accept even more good into your life.

If I can do it, so can you!

Chapter 10

Some Closing Thoughts

In closing I want to reiterate the importance of dealing with your grief early and head on during the period immediately following your wife's passing. While there are exceptions, the consequences of ignoring or delaying the process can be much more harmful in the long run than the actual grief itself.

On this topic, I like Mark Liebenow's post on The Good Men Project, *"Why We Need to Give Men Permission to Grieve"* on Sept. 3, 2015. (https://goodmenproject.com/author/mark-liebenow/)

"Grief is not a wound that will heal on its own. It will not fade away over time... grief is going to hang around until we open its box and deal with its contents... there are really good reasons for not delaying grief:

1.   Grief won't go away until it's faced.

2.   People are willing to help us now. They won't be later...

"...In the minds of most people, time equates to recovery, whether or not we've actually done any grieving... People expect us to grieve in the first month, and be moody, angry, sad, and depressed. We have their permission to cry and fall apart, and no one thinks less of us... people will respond with compassion... Then they go back to their busy lives, and we're left on our own... We need to set our pride aside and let people help..."

You may discover, as I did, that you will continue to process your grief for years after her passing. It will still be difficult; but, you will begin to feel that your progress is real and lasting.

After a year, I found that my thoughts about my wife were more sporadic, less painful, and more along the lines of remembering a very special and close friend who gave me many memorable experiences, lots of love, and the support I needed to become the person I am now. Occasionally the old pain and sorrow returns, but, it goes less deep and lasts an abbreviated period. The real test will come next Christmas.

I plan to have many distractions, so I can hopefully not sink into a deep depression again.

The following Caring Bridge entry demonstrates my state of mind at one year after her death.

Caring Bridge #34: Memorial & Spreading Ashes
By Fred Colby, June 6, 2016

My daughters, their families, and I took a trip to the mountains this past week to remember Theresa and to spread her ashes. It was a painful but therapeutic experience which fulfilled her wishes. Theresa loved going up to this idyllic location where we could enjoy some time together and with our families. This beautiful quiet setting is conducive to deep thinking and real conversations. Theresa would join me for walks, sit on the porch swing, look for wildlife and of course work on some of her stamping projects while there.

During our little informal ceremony, I read something that I had written which encapsulated my thoughts on what this all meant to me: "When we let go of these ashes, we are not letting go of Mama Theresa - what we are letting go of is the idea that she is with us physically, of the idea that she could walk in from the next room at any moment. We do continue to hold on to her memory and the love she expressed to each of us, and the great example she left us. We continue to remember and to love her always. That, we will never let go of."

After spreading the ashes at several spots around the ranch (the picture shows my grandson helping me to pour some into the river) we replaced the ashes in the urn with mementos of Theresa, symbolizing the letting go of the material body and replacing it with our ongoing memories of her. We are fast coming up on the one-year mark since her passing, so the timing of this seemed very appropriate.

I am grateful to have such great daughters, sons-in-laws, and grandchildren to support me and each other through this process.

Paula Stephens published the following on **Crazygoodgrief.com** which struck true for me, *"Explain to GRIEF that... it is only a small piece of all the incredible memories and experiences that make up your life. Let it know that it is welcome at the table because it is very important to understanding the entire texture of your life. But also, let GRIEF know that it is not allowed to come in and scare away all the other beautiful parts that make you an effervescent, shining being. Nor is GRIEF allowed to take joy, happiness, and zest for living hostage."*

If you are in the earliest stages of your grief and you are one of those people who read the Introduction and the Conclusion before you buy a book, you may think, "That won't happen to me!" I am sorry to tell you that it probably will. So, don't put off confronting it and getting through your grief. You cannot defeat it, but, you can survive it. The more directly you address your grief, the more likely you are to come out of this intact and ready to continue living a full and fruitful rest of your life.

Your new life will likely have several periods of redefining yourself. This is not running away from your wife so much as it is the process of creating a new and better version of you which is prepared to go forward with or without a new partner. You may as well realize this and work towards being able to once again enjoy life fully.

Like me, your wife may have completed and defined you. With her now gone, you must reimagine who you are without her in your life. Try to retain the best of what she instilled in you and continue to grow into a new and better you. As the first anniversary of my wife's death approached, I realized this redefining process will be ongoing, not a one and done thing.

I no longer fear this transition. I am even willing to embrace it. Fear and uncertainty are no longer prevalent forces in my life; but, grief is still present. This creates a sadness in my life that I know may never dispel. I escape it for longer periods of time now, but, know that it can return at any moment.

I know that I must continue this journey and make the most of the time I have left to enjoy the blessings that remain in my life.

As your brother in grief, I join all the widowers out there who have survived this ordeal in one piece, sending you support as you endeavor to survive your own grief experience. We are out there in greater numbers than ever, and due to our growing empathetic abilities, we are ready to help you if you ask for it.

So, please, ask!

ENDNOTES

[1] Scott Campbell and D. Phyllis Silverman, *Widower: When Men are Left Alone* (New York, Prentice Hall, 1996), page 75

[2] Alan Wolfelt, PhD, Center for Loss & Life Transition; www.centerforloss.com/

[3] Campbell, Ibid, page 170

[4] Ruth Davis Konigsberg, "5 Surprising Truths About Grief", AARP; https://www.aarp.org/caregiving/basics/info-2017/truth-about-grief.html

[5] George A. Bonanno, *The Other Side of Sadness: What the New Science of Bereavement Tells Us About Life After Loss* (New York, Basic Books, 2009)

[6] Helen Stang, "5 Stages of grief: Are They Real," Mindfulness & Grief; http://mindfulnessandgrief.com/5-stages-of-grief/

[7] Nanci Hellmich, "Feeling lonely? It may increase risk of early death," USA Today, February 17, 2014; https://www.usatoday.com/story/news/nation/2014/02/17/loneliness-seniors-early-death/5534323/

[8] Romeo Vitale, "Grief, Loneliness, and Losing a Spouse," Psychology Today, March 16, 2015; https://www.psychologytoday.com/blog/media-spotlight/201503/grief-loneliness-and-losing-spouse

[9] Konigsberg, Ibid

REFERENCES

Ames, Ed, *A Handbook for Widowers*, Omaha, NE, Centering Corp., 2004.

Bonanno, George A., *The Other Side of Sadness: What the New Science of Bereavement Tells Us About Life After Loss*, New York, Basic Books, 2009.

Campbell, Scott and D. Phyllis Silverman, 1996, *Widower: When Men are Left Alone*, New York, Prentice Hall, 1996.

Doka, Kenneth J. and Joyce D Davidson with foreword by Jack Gordon, *Living with Grief: Who We Are, How We Grieve*, New York, Routledge, 1998.

Doka, Kenneth J. with T. Martin, foreword by Dr. Therese A. Rando, *Men Don't Cry, Women Do: Transcending Gender Stereotypes on Grief*, Philadelphia, PA, Brunner/Mazel, 2000.

Frey, William H., *Crying: The Mystery of Tears*, New York, HarperCollins, 1985.

Golden, Thomas R., LCSW, *Swallowed by a Snake*, Gaithersburg, MD, Golden Healing Publishing, 1996.

Golden, Thomas R., LCSW, *The Way Men Heal,* Gaithersburg, MD, Golden Healing Publishing, 2013.

Golden, Thomas R. and James E. Miller, *When a Man Faces Grief, A Man You Know is Grieving*, Fort Wayne, IN, Willowgreen Publishing, 1998.

Konigsberg, Ruth Davis, *The Truth About Grief: The Myth of Its Five Stages and The New Science of Loss*, New York, Simon & Schuster, 2011.

Kennedy, Alexandra, MA, MFT, *The Infinite Thread: Healing Relationships Beyond Loss*, Hillsboro, OR, 2001.

Levang, Elizabeth, Ph.D., *When Men Grieve: Why Men Grieve Differently and How You Can Help,* Minneapolis, Minnesota, Fairview Press, 1998.

Lewis, C.S., *A Grief Observed*, New York, HarperCollins, 1961.

Page, Patrick W., *Cowbells and Courage*, Centering Corp., Omaha, NE, 2003.

Petrie, Dr. Ronald G., *Into the Cave: When Men Grieve*, Morrison, CO, One to Another, 2001.

Rando, Therese A., Ph.D., BCETS, BCBT, *How to Go On Living When Someone You Love Dies*, New York, Bantam Books, 1991.

Schaefer, Gerald J. with Tom Bekkers, MSW, APSW, *The Widower's Toolbox,* Far Hills, New Jersey, New Horizon's Press, 2010.